GRADE
5

Common CORE Mathematics

Practice at 3 Levels ● ● ●

W9-BDO-604

Table of Contents

Using This Book

What Is the Common Core?

The Common Core State Standards are an initiative by the states to set shared, consistent, and clear expectations of what students are expected to learn, so teachers and parents know what they need to do to help them. The standards are designed to be rigorous and pertinent to the real world. They reflect the knowledge and skills that our young people need for success in college and careers.

What Are the Intended Outcomes of Common Core?

The goal of the Common Core Standards is to facilitate the following competencies.

Students will:
- demonstrate independence;
- build strong content knowledge;
- respond to the varying demands of audience, task, purpose, and discipline;
- comprehend as well as critique;
- value evidence;
- use technology and digital media strategically and capably;
- come to understand other perspectives and cultures.

What Does This Mean for You?

If your state has joined the Common Core State Standards Initiative, then as a teacher you are required to incorporate these standards into your lesson plans. Your students may need targeted practice in order to meet grade-level standards and expectations and thereby be promoted to the next grade. This book is appropriate for on-grade-level students as well as for intervention, ELs, struggling readers, and special needs. To see if your state has joined the initiative, visit the Common Core States Standards Initiative website to view the most recent adoption map: http://www.corestandards.org/in-the-states.

What Does the Common Core Say Specifically About Math?

For math, the Common Core sets the following key expectations.

- Make sense of problems and persevere in solving them.
- Reason abstractly and quantitatively.
- Construct viable arguments and critique the reasoning of others.
- Model with mathematics.
- Use appropriate tools strategically.
- Attend to precision.
- Look for and make use of structure.
- Look for and express regularity in repeated reasoning.

How Does Common Core Mathematics Help My Students?

- **Mini-lesson for each unit** introduces
  Common Core math skills and concepts.

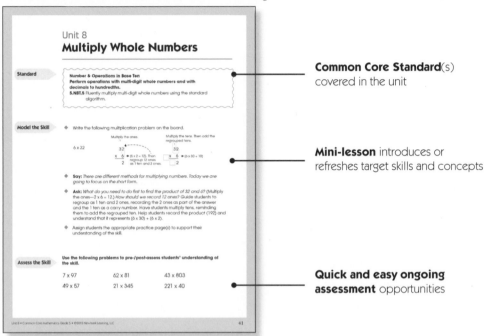

Common Core Standard(s)
covered in the unit

Mini-lesson introduces or
refreshes target skills and concepts

**Quick and easy ongoing
assessment** opportunities

- **Four practice pages** with three levels of differentiated practice,
  and word problems follow each mini-lesson.

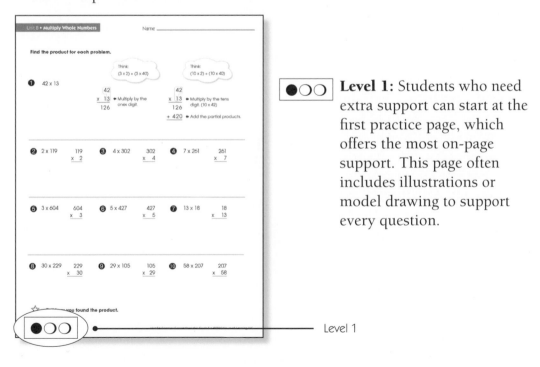

Level 1: Students who need
extra support can start at the
first practice page, which
offers the most on-page
support. This page often
includes illustrations or
model drawing to support
every question.

Level 1

Level 2: The second level of practice offers streamlined support features for the first few problems (illustrations, model drawing, or an algorithm reminder for support).

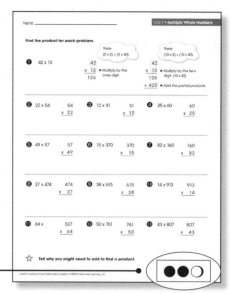

 Each practice page includes a bonus thinking-skills question so students can answer "How do you know?" to address Common Core Standards of Mathematical Practice and demonstrate their reasoning and understanding of the concept.

☆ **Tell how you used place value.**

Bonus Thinking Skills question on each practice page

Level 3: The third practice page does not offer on-page support and depicts how students are expected to be able to perform at this grade level, whether in class or in testing.

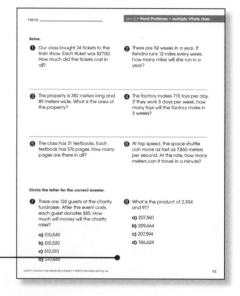

Level 3

Word Problems: Each unit ends with a page of short answer and multiple-choice word problems so students are challenged to marry their computation skills with their quantitative-reasoning and problem-solving skills and grow more familiar with the types of problems they will encounter on standardized tests.

Word Problem Page

Common Core Standards Alignment Chart • Grade 5

Units	5.OA.1	5.OA.2	5.OA.3	5.NBT.1	5.NBT.2	5.NBT.3	5.NBT.4	5.NBT.5	5.NBT.6	5.NBT.7	5.NF.1	5.NF.2	5.NF.3	5.NF.4	5.NF.5	5.NF.6	5.NF.7	5.MD.1	5.MD.2	5.MD.3	5.MD.4	5.MD.5	5.G.1	5.G.2	5.G.3	5.G.4
Operations & Algebraic Thinking																										
Unit 1: Order of Operations	✔																									
Unit 2: Write and Interpret Expressions		✔																								
Unit 3: Patterns and Ordered Pairs			✔																							
Number & Operations in Base Ten																										
Unit 4: Decimal Place Value				✔		✔																				
Unit 5: Powers of 10					✔																					
Unit 6: Compare Decimals						✔																				
Unit 7: Round Decimals							✔																			
Unit 8: Multiply Whole Numbers								✔																		
Unit 9: Divide by a One-Digit Divisor									✔																	
Unit 10: Divide by a Two-Digit Divisor									✔																	
Unit 11: Add and Subtract Decimals										✔																
Unit 12: Multiply Decimals										✔																
Unit 13: Divide Decimals										✔																
Number & Operations—Fractions																										
Unit 14: Add Fractions											✔	✔														
Unit 15: Subtract Fractions											✔	✔														
Unit 16: Multiply Whole Numbers/Fractions													✔	✔	✔											
Unit 17: Multiply Fractions													✔	✔	✔											
Unit 18: Multiply Mixed Numbers													✔	✔	✔	✔	✔									
Unit 19: Divide Whole Numbers/Fractions																	✔									
Measurement & Data																										
Unit 20: Convert Among Metric Units																		✔								
Unit 21: Convert Among Customary Units																		✔								
Unit 22: Use Measurement Data																			✔							
Unit 23: Understand Volume																				✔	✔					
Unit 24: Find Volume																					✔	✔				
Geometry																										
Unit 25: Locate Points on Coordinate Plane																							✔	✔		
Unit 26: Graph Points on the Coordinate Plane																							✔	✔		
Unit 27: Classify Polygons																									✔	✔

Unit 1
Order of Operations

Standard

Operations & Algebraic Thinking
Write and interpret numerical expressions.
5.OA.1 Use parentheses, brackets, or braces in numerical expressions, and evaluate expressions with these symbols.

Model the Skill

Order of Operations

1. Simplify within parentheses.

2. Multiply and divide from left to right.

3. Add and subtract from left to right.

◆ Write the equation 6 – 4 = 2 on the board. **Say:** *This is an equation. It uses numbers and symbols and an equal sign.* Write the expression 6 – 4 on the board. **Say:** *This is an expression. How is this different from the equation?* (It does not have an equal sign or an answer.) *Today, we will be evaluating expressions. When you evaluate an expression, you find the solution.*

◆ Write the expression 7 x 9 – 4 on the board.

◆ **Ask:** *What do you notice about this expression?* (Possible answer: It has three numbers and two different operation symbols.) *To evaluate this expression, you complete the operations from left to right just as you read words in a sentence. What is 7 multiplied by 9?* (63) *Now you can subtract 4 to finish evaluating the expression. What is 63 minus 4?* (59)

◆ Assign students the appropriate practice page(s) to support their understanding of the skill.

Assess the Skill

Use the following problems to pre-/post-assess students' understanding of the skill.

◆ Ask students to solve each problem.

36 ÷ 9 – 3	50 – 12 x 3	26 – 3 x (14 ÷ 2)
42 x 2 – 1	(8 + 17) x 3	(80 – 3) ÷ 11
63 ÷ (9 – 2)	32 ÷ 8 x 4	5 – 51 ÷ 17

Use the order of operations. Evaluate each expression.

> **Order of Operations**
> 1. Simplify within parentheses.
> 2. Multiply and divide from left to right.
> 3. Add and subtract from left to right.

1   5 x 6 – 4

    ↓   ↓

   30   – 4 = _____

2   32 ÷ 4 + 2

      ↓   ↓

   _____ + 2 = _____

---

3   36 ÷ 6 – 2

    ↓   ↓

   _____ – _____ = _____

4   36 ÷ (6 – 2)

    ↓   ↓

   _____ ÷ _____ = _____

---

5   40 ÷ 5 + 3

      ↓   ↓

   _____

6   3 x 48 ÷ (15 – 3)

      ↓   ↓

   _____

---

7   (25 – 5) x 4 ÷ 2

      ↓   ↓

   _____

8   64 ÷ (2 x 2) – 3

      ↓   ↓

   _____

☆   **Circle the operation you completed first to solve Problem 8.**

    ●○○

Name _____

Use the order of operations. Evaluate each expression.

> **Order of Operations**
> 1. Simplify within parentheses.
> 2. Multiply and divide from left to right.
> 3. Add and subtract from left to right.

1 $5 \times (6 - 3)$

2 $24 \times (4 - 2)$

3 $32 \div (8 - 4)$

4 $28 \div (7 - 3)$

5 $7 \times (7 - 3)$

6 $56 \div (11 - 3)$

7 $3 + (4 \times 3)$

8 $40 + (72 \div 9) \div 8$

9 $23 + (30 \div 10) \times 4$

10 $(24 - 16) \div 8$

11 $32 - 16 \div 8$

12 $4 \times 5 \div 2 - 1$

☆ **Tell how evaluating an expression with parentheses affects the solution.**

Use the order of operations. Evaluate each expression.

1 $(17 \times 2) \div (16 \div 8)$ **2** $(25 - 1) + (7 \times 2)$ **3** $(5 \times 5) \times (6 - 2)$ **4** $8 \times 8 - 9 \times 7$

5 $(4 \times 8) - (9 + 7)$ **6** $(2 \times 8) - 9 + 7$ **7** $426 \div 3 \times 10$ **8** $183 - 3 \times 50$

9 $56 + 4 \times 6$ **10** $178 - (3 \times 9)$ **11** $5 \times (20 - 3) + 8$ **12** $49 \div 2 + 5$

13 $4 \times 8 + (19 - 3)$ **14** $190 \div 2 - 2$ **15** $76 + 14 \times 2$ **16** $24 \times 4 \div 2 \times 3$

17 $56 - (5 \times 5 + 5)$ **18** $88 - 11 \div 11$ **19** $12 \times 5 + 6 \times 3$ **20** $135 \div 9 - 8 \div 2$

 Write an explanation of how you evaluated Problem 17.

Name _____

Solve.

1 Hilary has six times as many apples as James. James has 3 green apples and 4 red apples. How many apples does Hilary have?

2 Kendall has three fewer pencils than Lara. Lara has twice as many pencils as Stephanie. If Stephanie has 10 pencils, how many pencils does Kendall have?

3 There are 13 cars parked in the lot on Wednesday. There are 4 more cars parked on Thursday. There are 5 times that amount on Saturday. How many cars are parked on Saturday?

4 Jaden has 56 baseball cards in a pile. Jaden divides the cards evenly into four albums and then buys 2 more cards for each album. How many cards does Jaden have in all?

5 Brady has 3 dozen eggs. He uses 6 eggs to bake some muffins. Then he uses three times that amount to make omelettes. How many eggs does Brady have left?

6 There are 4 windows in the living room. Each window has 1 set of blinds and 2 panels of curtains. The blinds cost $20 each. Each curtain panel costs $28. How much do the window treatments cost?

Circle the letter for the correct answer.

7 $48 \div 8 - 2 = ?$

   a) 2

   b) 4

   c) 6

   d) 8

8 $90 \times 7 - 4 \times 50 \div 2 = ?$

   a) 6,750

   b) 215

   c) 530

   d) 3,375

Unit 2
Write and Interpret Expressions

Operations & Algebraic Thinking
Write and interpret numerical expressions.
5.OA.2 Write simple expressions that record calculations with numbers, and interpret numerical expressions without evaluating them. For example, express the calculation "add 8 and 7, then multiply by 2" as 2 x (8 + 7). Recognize that 3 x (18,932 + 921) is three times as large as 18,932 + 921, without having to calculate the indicated sum or product.

Model the Skill

◆ Write the equation 6 + 7 = 13 on the board. **Say:** *This is an equation. It uses numbers and symbols and an equal sign.* Write the expression 6 + 7 on the board. **Ask:** *How is this different from the equation?* (It does not have an equal sign or a sum.) *This is an expression. An expression is similar to an equation in that it uses numbers and symbols, but it does not include an equal sign or an answer. We will be writing expressions but not solving the problems.*

◆ Write "six times as large as 4" on the board and read it aloud.

◆ **Say:** *Think about the statement "six times as large as." Does that wording indicate that the values should be added or subtracted?* (no) Guide students to see that the values need to be multiplied. Allow them to use counters or draw a picture to see the operation.
Ask: *What expression matches the statement?* (6 x 4)

◆ Assign students the appropriate practice page(s) to support their understanding of the skill. Be sure to discuss what alternate phrases that might be used to indicate each operation.

Assess the Skill

Use the following problems to pre-/post-assess students' understanding of the skill.

◆ Ask students to write an expression for each statement.

8 more than 17

15 less than 24

9 less than the product of 5 and 7

13 more than the quotient of 51 divided by 3

Circle the matching expression for each statement.

1 4 times as large as 16

$$4 + 16$$
$$16 - 4$$
$$4 \times 16$$
$$16 \div 4$$

2 the difference between 6 and 11

$$6 + 11$$
$$11 - 6$$
$$6 \times 11$$
$$11 \div 6$$

3 5 less than 8

$$8 + 5$$
$$8 - 5$$
$$8 \times 5$$
$$8 \div 5$$

4 8 times the amount of 4

$$4 + 8$$
$$8 - 4$$
$$4 \times 8$$
$$8 \div 4$$

5 3 increased by 4

$$3 + 4$$
$$3 - 4$$
$$3 \times 4$$
$$3 \div 4$$

6 9 decreased by 6

$$9 + 6$$
$$9 - 6$$
$$6 \times 9$$
$$9 \div 6$$

☆ **Circle the problems where the operation is subtraction.**

●○○

Name _____

Write an expression to describe each statement.

1 5 times the difference between 8 and 6

5 ◯ (8 ◯ 6)

2 9 times the sum of 3 and 5

9 ◯ (5 ◯ 3)

3 10 times the difference between 12 and 7

10 ◯ (12 ◯ 7)

---

4 8 less than the product of 4 and 6

(☐ x ☐) – ☐

5 16 more than the product of 3 and 7

(☐ x ☐) + ☐

6 the product of 5 and 9 decreased by 7

(☐ x ☐) – ☐

---

7 the sum of 2 and 4 increased by 12

8 the quotient of 30 divided by 5 increased by 14

9 7 more than the product of 8 and 6

---

10 the product of 12 and 3 decreased by 6

11 11 more than nine times the amount of ten

12 the difference between 16 and 4, divided by 6

 Tell how you know when to multiply.

Name _____

Write an expression for each statement.

1 add 12 and 9, then divide by 3

_____

2 subtract 9 from 17, then multiply by 3

_____

3 four times the sum of 7 and 9

_____

4 the product of 6 and 7 plus 5

_____

5 7 more than the product of 8 and 4

_____

6 9 less than the product of 5 and 7

_____

7 the quotient of 28 divided by four increased by 3

_____

8 subtract 7 from the sum of 28 and 2

_____

9 5 more than the product of 9 and 19

_____

10 the quotient of 14 divided by 7 increased by 11

_____

11 6 times the product of 2 and 5

_____

12 3 times the difference between 42 and 30

_____

13 the difference between 17 and 50 increased by 7

_____

14 the product of 9 and 8 divided by 6

_____

15 the sum of 14 and 22 divided by 9

_____

16 the difference between 34 and 42 divided by 4

_____

17 subtract 9 from 17, then multiply by 4

_____

18 increase 23 by 7, then divide by 5

_____

19 decrease the product of 13 and 2 by 8

_____

20 multiply the sum of 45 and 11 by 2

_____

 Explain how you wrote the expression for Problem 20.

Write an expression for each statement. Then solve.

1 5 times the difference between 19 and 13

2 the product of 12 and 5 decreased by 17

3 the quotient of 28 divided by 7 increased by 4

4 the sum of 24 and 12 divided by 9

5 Multiply the sum of 11 and 4 by 3. Then add 5.

6 Add the product of 5 and 6 with the product of 3 and 7.

Circle the letter for the correct answer.

7 Multiply the difference of 39 and 30 by 5, then add 6.

a) $5 \times (39 - 30) + 6$
b) $39 - 30 \times 5 + 6$
c) $(39 - 30) \times (5 + 6)$
d) $(5 \times 30) - 39 + 6$

8 Which statement best describes the following equation?

$(30 + 6) \div 9 + 3$

a) 30 increased by 6 divided by the sum of 9 and 3
b) the sum of 30 and 6 divided by the sum of 9 and 3
c) the sum of 30 and 6 divided by 9, then increased by 3
d) 6 more than 30, decreased by 9 plus 3

Unit 3
Patterns and Ordered Pairs

Operations & Algebraic Thinking
Analyze patterns and relationships.
5.OA.3 Generate two numerical patterns using two given rules. Identify apparent relationships between corresponding terms. Form ordered pairs consisting of corresponding terms from the two patterns, and graph the ordered pairs on a coordinate plane.

Model the Skill

◆ Write the rule "Add 5" on the board and read it aloud. Then draw the following pattern table.

x add 1	1	2	3	4	5
y add 5	5	10			

◆ **Say:** *Today we are going to extend number patterns. The rule is given. If you add 5 to 5, what is the sum?* (10) *What is the sum of 10 and 5?* (15) *If you continue the pattern, what is the last number in the pattern?* (25)

◆ Guide students to see the relationship between each number *x* in the top row and each number *y* in the bottom row. **Ask:** *How would you describe the relationship between the top and bottom rows? Does it follow a pattern?* (yes, multiply by 5)

◆ **Say:** *So* y = 5x. *We can graph this on the coordinate plane.*

◆ Assign students the appropriate practice page(s) to support their understanding of the skill.

Assess the Skill

Use the following problems to pre-/post-assess students' understanding of the skill.

◆ Ask students to complete the following pattern tables. Then list the ordered pairs.

x add 1	y add 3
1	3
2	6
3	
4	

x subtract 1	y subtract 3
6	18
5	

Complete each pattern.

Subtract 5	25	20	15		

Subtract 1	5	4			

❷

Add 2	Add 6
2	6
4	12

❸

Subtract 2	Subtract 4
10	20
8	16

Look for a relationship in the ordered pairs. Then write the rules.

❹

x	y
10	20
12	24
14	28
16	32

Relationship: _____

Rules: _____

_____

❺

x	y
30	5
24	4
18	3
12	2

Relationship: _____

Rules: _____

_____

 Tell how the patterns are related.

Name _____

Complete each pattern. Then write the ordered pairs in the table.

1

add 1	3	4	5	6	7
add 2	6	8			

x	y
3	6
4	8
5	
6	
7	

2

subtract 2	24	22	20		
subtract 1	12	11	10		

x	y
24	12
22	11
20	

3

add 1	1	2	3		
add 5	5	10	15		

x	y
1	
2	
3	

4

subtract 6	36	30	24		
subtract 4	24	20	16		

x	y
36	
30	

5

add 10	10			
add 20	20	40	60	

x	y

6

subtract 15	60	45	30		
subtract 5	40	35	30		

x	y
60	
45	
30	

7

add 10	10	20	30		
add 15	15	30	45		

x	y
10	
20	
30	

8

subtract 3	33	30	27		
subtract 1	12	11	10		

x	y

☆ **Tell about the relationship of the ordered pairs.**

Unit 3 • Common Core Mathematics Grade 5 • ©2012 Newmark Learning, LLC

Name _____

Follow the rules to find the missing values. Then write the ordered pairs.

1

x add 1	y add 3
1	3
2	6
3	
4	

(1, 3), (2, __),

(3, __), (__, __)

2

x add 4	y add 2
4	2
8	4
12	
16	

(4, __), (8, __),

(__ , __), (__ , __)

3

x subtract 1	y subtract 3
4	12
3	

(__, __), (__, __),

(__, __), (__, __)

4

x subtract 3	y subtract 1

(__, __), (__, __),

(__, __), (__, __)

5

x add 5	y add 10

(__, __), (__, __),

(__, __), (__, __)

6

x subtract 1	y subtract 10

(__, __), (__, __),

(__, __), (__, __)

7

x subtract 1	y subtract 3

(__, __), (__, __),

(__, __), (__, __)

8

x subtract 1	y subtract 3

(__, __), (__, __),

(__, __), (__, __)

9

x subtract 6	y subtract 2

(__, __), (__, __),

(__, __), (__, __)

10

x add 8	y subtract 4

(__, __), (__, __),

(__, __), (__, __)

 Tell how you know which numbers to write in the ordered pair.

Name _____

Look for a relationship in the ordered pairs. Then write the rules.

1

x	y
3	6
6	12
9	18
12	24

Relationship: _____

Rules: _____

_____

2

x	y
10	20
8	16
6	12
4	8

Relationship: _____

Rules: _____

_____

3

x	y
1	3
6	18
11	33
16	48

Relationship: _____

Rules: _____

_____

4

x	y
21	7
18	6
15	5
12	4

Relationship: _____

Rules: _____

_____

5

x	y
1	
2	
3	15
4	

Relationship: _____

Rules: _____

_____

6

x	y
24	6
20	

Relationship: _____

Rules: _____

_____

Circle the letter for the correct answer.

7 Which ordered pair belongs to this set?

(15, 12), (14, 11), (13, 10), _____

a) (16, 14)
b) (13, 10)
c) (12, 9)
d) (11, 8)

8 Which equation below describes the relationship between x and y?

a) $y = x + 3$
b) $y = x + 4$
c) $x = 2y + 1$
d) $y = 2x - 1$

x	y
4	7
5	9
6	11
7	

Unit 4
Decimal Place Value

Standard

Number & Operations in Base Ten
Understand the place value system.
5.NBT.1 Recognize that in a multi-digit number, a digit in one place represents
10 times as much as it represents in the place to its right and 1/10 of
what it represents in the place to its left.
5.NBT.3 Read, write, and compare decimals to thousandths.
a) Read and write decimals to thousandths using base-ten numerals,
number names, and expanded form.

Model the Skill

hundreds	tens	ones	.	tenths	hundredths	thousandths
			.			

◆ Draw a place value chart on the board.

◆ **Say:** *Look at the place value chart. How many places are shown on this
chart?* (6) *Which place is the greatest?* (hundreds) Point out the decimal
point and explain that three places are to the left of the decimal point and
three places are to the right of the decimal point.

◆ **Ask:** *How does the tens place compare to the ones place?* (The tens place
is 10 times more than the ones place.) Explain that each place is 1/10 of the
place to its left—the tenths place is 1/10 of the ones place. Have students
write the number "one hundred four and thirty-eight hundredths" in the place
value chart. Point out that **and** indicates there is a fraction of a number, or a
decimal amount, that follows the whole number portion.

◆ **Ask:** *How do we write one hundred four in the place value chart?* (1
in the hundreds, 0 in the tens, and 4 in the ones) *How do we write thirty-
eight hundredths in the place value chart?* (3 in the tenths place, 8 in the
hundredths place) Demonstrate how to use the numbers written in the chart to
write the standard form. (104.38) Have students look at the standard form and
say the number aloud, making sure that it matches the word form.

◆ Assign students the appropriate practice page(s) to support their
understanding of the skill.

Assess the Skill

**Use the following problems to pre-/post-assess students' understanding of
the skill.**

◆ Ask students to write the following decimals in standard, expanded, and
written form:
• sixty-five and eight-hundredths
• one hundred thirty and forty-four hundredths
• five hundred one and eighty-six thousandths

Name _____

Write each number as indicated. Use the place value chart to help you.

hundreds	tens	ones	.	tenths	hundredths	thousandths
			.			

1 one hundred three and nine-tenths

standard form: _____

2 forty and five hundred sixty-seven thousandths

standard form: _____

3 two and thirteen-hundredths

standard form: _____

4 18.06

written form: _____

5 10.13

written form: _____

6 140.5

expanded form: _____

☆ **Circle the decimal that shows thousandths.**

Read each number. Write its word name. Use the place value chart to help you.

hundreds	tens	ones	.	tenths	hundredths	thousandths
			.			

1 standard form: 24.76

expanded form: _____

written form: _____

2 standard form: 21.035

expanded form: _____

written form: _____

3 standard form: 400.04

expanded form: _____

written form: _____

4 standard form: 121.06

expanded form: _____

written form: _____

5 standard form: _____

expanded form: _____

written form: three hundred five and five tenths

6 standard form: _____

expanded form: _____

written form: seven hundred eighteen and twelve thousandths

7 standard form: _____

expanded form: $90 + 9 + \frac{8}{10} + \frac{3}{100}$

written form: _____

8 300.4

expanded form: _____

written form: _____

 Tell how place value helps you read and write a number.

Name _____

Complete the chart.

	Standard Form	Expanded Form	Written Form
1	6.17		
2		$30 + 5 + \frac{2}{10}$	
3		$4 + \frac{5}{10} + \frac{7}{100} + \frac{9}{1,000}$	
4			eight hundred two and six-hundredths
5	206.047		
6	74.21		
7	8.096		
8			twenty and sixty–two hundredths
9			ninety-five and four-tenths
10		$600 + 5 + \frac{3}{100}$	

 Tell how you know the value of each digit in a number.

Name _____

Solve.

1 Write 510.401 in expanded form.

2 Write three hundred fifty-two and four-tenths in standard form.

3 Write 10.7 in written form.

4 Write seven hundred one and one-thousandth in standard form.

5 Write $200 + 50 + 7 + \frac{5}{10} + \frac{7}{100} + \frac{2}{1,000}$ in written form.

6 Write nine hundred one and seventy-five thousandths in expanded form.

Circle the letter for the correct answer.

7 Which of the following shows 17.201 in expanded form?

 a) $17 + \frac{2}{10} + \frac{0}{100} + \frac{1}{1,000}$

 b) seventeen and two hundred and one thousandths

 c) $10 + 7 + \frac{2}{10} + \frac{1}{1,000}$

 d) seventeen and two-tenths and one thousandth

8 Which of the following shows nine hundred and fifty-two thousandths in standard form?

 a) 952,000

 b) 900.52

 c) 950.052

 d) 900.052

Unit 5
Powers of 10

Standard

Number & Operations in Base Ten
Understand the place value system.
5.NBT.2 Explain patterns in the number of zeros of the product when multiplying a number by powers of 10, and explain patterns in the placement of the decimal point when a decimal is multiplied or divided by a power of 10. Use whole-number exponents to denote powers of 10.

Model the Skill

◆ Write the following equations on the board.

$8 \times 1 = 8$		$8 \div 1 = 8$	
$8 \times 10 = 80$	$8 \times 10^1 = 80$	$8 \div 10 = 0.8$	$8 \div 10^1 = 0.8$
$8 \times 100 = 800$	$8 \times 10^2 = 800$	$8 \div 100 = 0.08$	$8 \div 10^2 = 0.08$
$8 \times 1,000 = 8,000$	$8 \times 10^3 = 8,000$	$8 \div 1,000 = 0.008$	$8 \div 10^3 = 0.008$

◆ Guide students to look at the pattern in the first two columns and connect it to place value.

◆ **Ask:** *What pattern do you see in the first column of equations?* (Possible answer: The product has the same number of zeros as the second factor.) Point out that you are moving the decimal point one place to the right when multiplying by 10, two places to the right when multiplying by 100 or 10^2, and three places to the right when multiplying by 1,000 or 10^3.

◆ **Ask:** *What is the product of 8 and 10^4?* (80,000)

◆ Guide students to look at the pattern in the second column and connect it to place value. **Ask:** *If you divide a whole number by 100 or 10^2, which direction will you move the decimal point and how many places will you move it?* (to the left, 2 places) *How many places to the left will you move the decimal point if you are dividing by 1,000 or 10^3?* (three)

◆ Assign students the appropriate practice page(s) to support their understanding of the skill.

Assess the Skill

Use the following problems to pre-/post-assess students' understanding of the skill.

$3.41 \times 10^2 = $ _____	$0.32 \times 10^4 = $ _____	$61.32 \div 10^2 = $ _____
$70.89 \times 10^3 = $ _____	$107.05 \times 10^3 = $ _____	$568.8 \div 10^4 = $ _____

Solve. Use patterns to help you.

1 $9 \times 1 = 9$

$9 \times 10 = 90$

$9 \times 100 = 900$

$9 \times 1,000 =$ _____

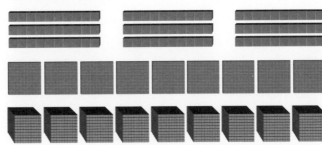

2 $9 \div 1 = 9$

$9 \div 10 = 0.9$

$9 \div 100 = 0.09$

$9 \div 1,000 =$ _____

3 $15 \times 10 = 150$

$15 \times 100 =$ _____

$15 \times 1,000 =$ _____

4 $72 \times 10 =$ _____

$72 \times 10^2 =$ _____

$72 \times 10^3 =$ _____

5 $40 \div 10 = 4$

$40 \div 100 =$ _____

$40 \div 1,000 =$ _____

6 $375 \div 10 = 37.5$

$375 \div 10^2 =$ _____

$375 \div 10^3 =$ _____

 Tell how you know how many zeros there should be in a product.

Name _____

Solve. Use patterns to help you.

1   2.1 x 10 = 21

     2.1 x 100 = 210

     2.1 x 1,000 = _____

2   5.0 ÷ 10 = 0.5

     5.0 ÷ 100 = 0.05

     5.0 ÷ 1,000 = _____

3   0.63 x 10 = 6.3

     0.63 x 100 = _____

     0.63 x 1,000 = _____

4   107 ÷ 10 = 10.7

     $107 ÷ 10^2$ = _____

     $107 ÷ 10^3$ = _____

5   432 x 10 = _____

     432 x 100 = _____

     432 x 1,000 = _____

6   9.08 x 10 = _____

     $9.08 × 10^2$ = _____

     $9.08 × 10^3$ = _____

7 $0.086 × 10^3$ = _____

8 $4.51 × 10^2$ = _____

9   0.33 ÷ 10 = _____

10   75,000 ÷ 100 = _____

11 $34.1 ÷ 10^3$ = _____

12 $9.28 × 10^4$ = _____

   Tell how the placement of the decimal point changes when a decimal is multiplied by 10^5.

Name _____

Solve.

1 943 x 10 = _____

943 x 100 = _____

943 x 1,000 = _____

2 712 x 10 = _____

712 x 100 = _____

712 x 1,000 = _____

3 63 ÷ 10 = _____

63 ÷ 10^2 = _____

63 ÷ 10^3 = _____

4 5,433 ÷ 10 = _____

5,433 ÷ 10^2 = _____

5,433 ÷ 10^3 = _____

5 432 ÷ 10^2 = _____

6 60.8 x 10 = _____

7 0.285 x 10^3 = _____

8 27 ÷ 10^3 = _____

9 251 ÷ 10 = _____

10 0.33 x 1,000 = _____

11 745,000 ÷ 10^3 = _____

12 278 ÷ 10^2 = _____

13 21.9 ÷ 10^3 = _____

14 97,004 ÷ 10^3 = _____

15 80.1 x 10^3 = _____

16 509.4 ÷ 10^3 = _____

17 650 ÷ 10^3 = _____

18 3.775 x 10^4 = _____

 Describe the pattern of zeros in the quotient when dividing by powers of 10.

Name _____

Solve. Use patterns to help you.

1 What is the product of 3.39 and 10^2?

2 What is the product of 542 and 10?

3 What is the product of 1.097 and 10^2?

4 What is the product of 200 and 10^2?

5 What is the quotient of 2,093 divided by 10^3?

6 What is the quotient of 70,098 divided by 10^2?

Circle the letter for the correct answer.

7 Which power of 10 multiplied by 7.8 is equal to 780?

    a) 10

    b) 10^2

    c) 10^3

    d) 1,000

8 What number when divided by 10^2 yields a quotient of 0.1?

    a) 1,000

    b) 100

    c) 10

    d) 1.0

Unit 6
Compare Decimals

Standard

Number & Operations in Base Ten
Understand the place value system.
5.NBT.3 Read, write, and compare decimals to thousandths.
a) Read and write decimals to thousandths using base-ten numerals, number names, and expanded form.
b) Compare two decimals to thousandths based on meanings of the digits in each place, using >, =, and < symbols to record the results of comparisons.

Model the Skill

◆ Draw a place value chart on the board.

ones	.	tenths	hundredths	thousandths
0	.	4		
0	.	6		

◆ **Say:** *A place value chart can help you compare decimals. What are the decimals shown in this first place value chart?* (0.4 and 0.6) *Both numbers have the same number of digits and the same number of decimal places. How do you compare these numbers?* (Possible answer: Start at the digit on the left and compare the digits in the same place. If the digits are the same, move to the next digit to the right. Then compare the two digits to see which is greater.) *Which number is greater?* (0.6) *If 0.6 is greater than 0.4, then 0.4 is less than 0.6.*

◆ Assign students the appropriate practice page(s) to support their understanding of the skill.

Assess the Skill

Use the following problems to pre-/post-assess students' understanding of the skill.

0.71 ◯ 0.18   3.59 ◯ 5.39

4.81 ◯ 4.18   20.5 ◯ 50.2

6.07 ◯ 6.71   0.598 ◯ 0.589

Name _____

Use a place value chart to compare numbers. Circle the correct statement.

1

ones	.	tenths	hundredths	thousandths
0	.	5		
0	.	7		

0.5 is greater than 0.7.

0.5 is less than 0.7.

2

ones	.	tenths	hundredths	thousandths
0	.	5	8	
0	.	5	9	

0.58 is greater than 0.59.

0.58 is less than 0.59.

3

ones	.	tenths	hundredths	thousandths
0	.	0	9	4
0	.	0	4	9

0.094 is greater than 0.049.

0.094 is less than 0.049.

4

ones	.	tenths	hundredths	thousandths
0	.	2	1	8
0	.	3	1	8

0.218 is greater than 0.318.

0.218 is less than 0.318.

5

ones	.	tenths	hundredths	thousandths
0	.	0	7	3
0	.	0	1	3

0.073 is greater than 0.013.

0.073 is less than 0.013.

6

ones	.	tenths	hundredths	thousandths
1	.	2	1	2
1	.	0	2	1

1.212 is greater than 1.021.

1.212 is less than 1.021.

 Tell how you use place value to compare numbers.

Unit 6 • Common Core Mathematics Grade 5 • ©2012 Newmark Learning, LLC

Name _____

Use a place value chart to compare numbers.
Write >, <, or = to complete each statement.

ones	.	tenths	hundredths	thousandths
2	.	9		
3	.	2		

> is greater than
< is less than
= is equal to

1   2.9 ◯ 3.2

2   1.76 ◯ 1.67

3   2.05 ◯ 2.11

4   31.08 ◯ 3.108

5   1.01 ◯ 1.1

6   5.927 ◯ 5.927

7   3.95 ◯ 4.35

8   0.86 ◯ 0.87

9   2.9 ◯ 2.6

10   6.013 ◯ 6.08

 Tell how you know when two numbers are equal.

Name _____

Use the symbols for greater than (>) or less than (<) to compare the numbers.

1   8.92 ◯ 8.9

2   8.92 ◯ 9.089

3   8.092 ◯ 8.9

4   8.92 ◯ 9.089

5   8.9 ◯ 9.089

6   8.092 ◯ 8.092

7   8.9 ◯ 9.089

8   8.09 ◯ 0.89

9   7.45 ◯ 7.54

10 2.3 ◯ 3.2

11 1.9 ◯ 1.09

12 0.68 ◯ 0.608

13 4.05 ◯ 4.14

14 5.2 ◯ 5.02

15 7.063 ◯ 7.063

16 9.2 ◯ 0.92

☆   **Tell how you use a place value chart to compare numbers.**

Solve.

1 Write a decimal that is less than 6.73.

2 Write a decimal that is greater than 0.04.

3 Write a decimal that is less than 5.89 and greater than 4.27.

4 Write a decimal that is greater than 3.3 and less than 3.73.

5 Tom paid $4.78 for his sandwich. Alicia paid $7.48 for a salad. Who paid more for lunch?

6 Marina bought 0.68 pound of American cheese and 0.82 pound of cheddar cheese. Which package of cheese weighed more?

Circle the letter for the correct answer.

7 Which statement is true?

a) 4.75 < 4.857 < 4.589

b) 4.75 < 4.589 < 4.857

c) 4.857 > 4.589 > 4.75

d) 4.589 < 4.75 < 4.857

8 Which statement is false?

a) 0.23 < 0.52 < 0.6

b) 1.7 < 2.1 < 4.3

c) 6.17 > 5.7 > 5.8

d) 0.9 > 0.89 > 0.869

Unit 7
Round Decimals

Standard

Number & Operations in Base Ten
Understand the place value system.
5.NBT.4 Use place value understanding to round decimals to any place.

Model the Skill

◆ Draw the following number line on the board.

◆ **Ask:** *How can you use a number line to help you round numbers?* (Find the number on the line and see which whole number it is closer to.) *How can you find 4.2 on the number line?* (Find 4 and move two marks to the right.) Guide students to make a dot where 4.2 is on the number line and determine which whole number it is closer to. (4)

◆ **Say:** *You can also round numbers by looking at the digit to the right of the digit you are rounding to. When rounding to the nearest whole number, which digit will you look at?* (the one in the tenths place) *What digit is in the tenths place of 4.2?* (2) Review with students that if a digit is less than 5, the digit you are rounding to stays the same. If it is 5 or greater, the digit you are rounding to increases by one.

◆ Assign students the appropriate practice page(s) to support their understanding of the skill.

Assess the Skill

Use the following problems to pre-/post-assess students' understanding of the skill.

◆ Ask students to round each number to the nearest one, tenths, or hundredths place.

0.71	4.18	3.59	50.2
0.18	6.07	5.39	0.598
4.81	6.71	20.5	0.589

Round to the nearest whole number. Use the number line to help.

1 4.8 rounds to _____

2 36.6 rounds to _____

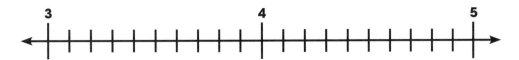

3 25.3 rounds to _____

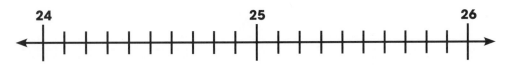

4 4.1 rounds to _____

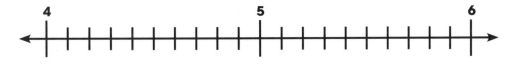

5 3.5 rounds to _____

6 38.9 rounds to _____

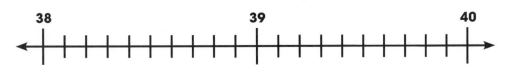

☆ **Tell how to use a number line to round decimals to the nearest whole number.**

Name _____

Round each number to the nearest tenth. Use the number line to help.

❶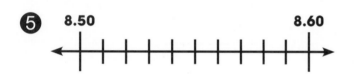

8.54 rounds to _____

❷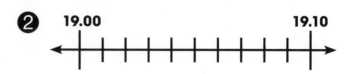

19.08 rounds to _____

❸

8.50   5.20   5.30

5.27 rounds to _____

❹

61.80   61.90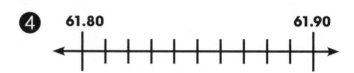

61.85 rounds to _____

❺

8.50   8.60

8.56 rounds to _____

❻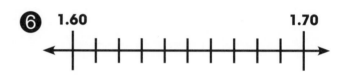

1.60   1.70

1.638 rounds to _____

❼

15.06 rounds to _____

❽

20.372 rounds to _____

❾

6.488 rounds to _____

❿

0.819 rounds to _____

 Tell how to use place value to round to the nearest tenth.

Round each number to the nearest hundredth. Use the number line to help.

1 3.450   3.460

3.459 rounds to _____

2 0.290   0.300

0.295 rounds to _____

3 40.261 rounds to _____

4 61.895 rounds to _____

5 8.533 rounds to _____

6 81.406 rounds to _____

7 7.602 rounds to _____

8 0.885 rounds to _____

9 0.967 rounds to _____

10 1.094 rounds to _____

11 1.059 rounds to _____

12 4.509 rounds to _____

 Tell how rounding to the nearest hundredth is like rounding to the nearest tenth.

Name _____

Solve.

1 What is 31.75 rounded to the nearest tenth?

2 What is 1.49 rounded to the nearest tenth?

3 What is 20.06 rounded to the nearest tenth?

4 What is 98.044 rounded to the nearest hundredth?

5 What is 5.197 rounded to the nearest tenth?

6 What is 76.975 rounded to the nearest hundredth?

Circle the letter for the correct answer.

7 If you were rounding 36.842 to the nearest tenth, which digit would you use to round the decimal?

a) 2

b) 4

c) 6

d) 8

8 If you rounded 0.587 to the nearest hundredth, what digit would be in the hundredths place?

a) 9

b) 8

c) 6

d) 0

Unit 8
Multiply Whole Numbers

Standard

Number & Operations in Base Ten
Perform operations with multi-digit whole numbers and with decimals to hundredths.
5.NBT.5 Fluently multiply multi-digit whole numbers using the standard algorithm.

Model the Skill

◆ Write the following multiplication problem on the board.

Multiply the ones.

Multiply the tens. Then add the regrouped tens.

6×32

$$\begin{array}{r} \overset{1}{3}2 \\ \times\ 6 \\ \hline 2 \end{array}$$ ← ($6 \times 2 = 12$) Then regroup 12 ones as 1 ten and 2 ones.

$$\begin{array}{r} \overset{1}{3}2 \\ \times\ 6 \\ \hline \boxed{\ }2 \end{array}$$ ← ($6 \times 30 + 10$)

◆ **Say:** *There are different methods for multiplying numbers. Today we are going to focus on the short form.*

◆ **Ask:** *What do you need to do first to find the product of 32 and 6?* (Multiply the ones—2 x 6 = 12.) *How should we record 12 ones?* Guide students to regroup as 1 ten and 2 ones, recording the 2 ones as part of the answer and the 1 ten as a carry number. Have students multiply tens, reminding them to add the regrouped ten. Help students record the product (192) and understand that it represents (6 x 30) + (6 x 2).

◆ Assign students the appropriate practice page(s) to support their understanding of the skill.

Assess the Skill

Use the following problems to pre-/post-assess students' understanding of the skill.

7 x 97	62 x 81	43 x 803
49 x 57	21 x 345	221 x 40

Name _____

Find the product for each problem.

Think:
(3 x 2) + (3 x 40)

Think:
(10 x 2) + (10 x 40)

1   42 x 13

```
  42
x 13   ← Multiply by the
 126      ones digit.
```

```
   42
 x 13   ← Multiply by the tens
  126      digit. (10 x 42)
+ 420   ← Add the partial products.
```

---

2 2 x 119   119
                    x   2

3 4 x 302   302
                    x   4

4 7 x 261   261
                    x   7

---

5 3 x 604   604
                    x   3

6 5 x 427   427
                    x   5

7 13 x 18   18
                    x 13

---

8 30 x 229   229
                    x 30

9 29 x 105   105
                    x 29

10 58 x 207   207
                    x 58

☆ **Tell how you found the product.**

Find the product for each problem.

Think:
(5 x 2) + (5 x 30)

Think:
(20 x 2) + (20 x 30)

1 32 x 25

```
  32
x 25   ← Multiply by the
────      ones digit.
 160
```

```
  32
x 25   ← Multiply by the tens
────      digit. (20 x 32)
 160
+640   ← Add the partial products.
```

---

2 22 x 54
```
   54
x  22
```

3 12 x 31
```
   31
x  12
```

4 25 x 60
```
   60
x  25
```

---

5 49 x 57
```
   57
x  49
```

6 15 x 370
```
  370
x  15
```

7 82 x 160
```
  160
x  82
```

---

8 27 x 474
```
  474
x  27
```

9 38 x 615
```
  615
x  38
```

10 14 x 913
```
  913
x  14
```

---

11 64 x 327
```
  327
x  64
```

12 50 x 761
```
  761
x  50
```

13 43 x 807
```
  807
x  43
```

 Tell why you might need to add to find a product.

Name _____

Find the product for each problem.

1   53
    x 56

2   85
    x 32

3   50
    x 28

4   96
    x 45

5   73
    x 16

6   75
    x 22

7   49
    x 19

8   88
    x 27

9   233
    x 26

10   445
    x 62

11   203
    x 11

12   340
    x 47

13   313
    x 42

14   175
    x 68

15   593
    x 31

16   192
    x 52

17   771
    x 21

18   842
    x 17

19   253
    x 31

20   703
    x 12

21   336
    x 30

22   405
    x 26

23   93
    x 79

24   919
    x 37

☆ **Explain how you use place value when you multiply.**

Name _____

Solve.

1 Our class bought 24 tickets to the train show. Each ticket was $27.00. How much did the tickets cost in all?

2 There are 52 weeks in a year. If Kendra runs 12 miles every week, how many miles will she run in a year?

3 The property is 382 meters long and 89 meters wide. What is the area of the property?

4 The factory workers make 715 toys per day. If they work 5 days per week, how many toys will the workers make in 3 weeks?

5 The class has 31 textbooks. Each textbook has 576 pages. How many pages are there in all?

6 At top speed, the space shuttle can move as fast as 7,860 meters per second. At this rate, how many meters can it travel in a minute?

Circle the letter for the correct answer.

7 There are 124 guests at the charity fund-raiser. Each guest donates $85 to the charity. How much will money will the charity raise?

a) $10,540

b) $10,520

c) $10,510

d) $10,440

8 What is the product of 2,304 and 91?

a) 207,360

b) 209,664

c) 207,594

d) 186,624

Unit 9
Divide by a One-Digit Divisor

Standard

Number & Operations in Base Ten
Perform operations with multi-digit whole numbers and with decimals to hundredths.
5.NBT.6 Find whole-number quotients of whole numbers with up to four-digit dividends and two-digit divisors, using strategies based on place value, the properties of operations, and/or the relationship between multiplication and division. Illustrate and explain the calculation by using equations, rectangular arrays, and/or area models.

Model the Skill

Think:
$4\overline{)9}$

$$\begin{array}{r} 2 \\ 4\overline{)96} \\ 80 \end{array}$$ ← Divide tens.

Then multiply.

$(20 \times 4 = 80)$

Think:
$4\overline{)16}$

$$\begin{array}{r} 2 \\ 4\overline{)96} \\ -80 \\ \hline 16 \end{array}$$ ← Subtract. $(96 - 80 = 16)$

← Divide ones.

$$\begin{array}{r} 24 \\ 4\overline{)96} \\ -80 \\ \hline 16 \\ -16 \\ \hline 0 \end{array}$$

← Multiply. $(4 \times 4 = 16)$
← Subtract. $(16 - 16 = 0)$

◆ **Ask:** *What is the quotient of 96 divided by 4?* (24)

◆ **Ask:** *How do you know?* (Possible answer: I divided the tens and the ones column in the dividend and found the quotient.) *How can you use multiplication to check division?* (Possible answer: Multiply the quotient by the divisor and see if you get the dividend.)

◆ Assign students the appropriate practice page(s) to support their understanding of the skill.

Assess the Skill

Use the following problems to pre-/post-assess students' understanding of the skill.

$98 \div 7$	$620 \div 8$	$803 \div 4$
$570 \div 6$	$2,345 \div 5$	$5,067 \div 9$

Name  _____

Find the quotient for each problem. Draw a picture.

1   27 ÷ 3   ← quotient

$$3\overline{)27}$$

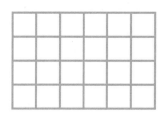

2   24 ÷ 4   ← quotient

$$4\overline{)24}$$

3   180 ÷ 6   ← quotient

$$6\overline{)180}$$

4   305 ÷ 5   ← quotient

$$5\overline{)305}$$

5   1,442 ÷ 7   ← quotient

$$7\overline{)1,442}$$

    Look at the Problem 4. Circle the divisor. Underline the dividend.

Name _____

Divide. Show your work.

1   726 ÷ 3 = _____

$\begin{array}{r} 2 \\ 3\overline{)726} \\ -600 \\ \hline 126 \end{array}$ ← Divide hundreds. ← Multiply. ← Then subtract.	$\begin{array}{r} 24 \\ 3\overline{)726} \\ -600 \\ \hline 126 \\ -120 \\ \hline 6 \end{array}$ ← Divide tens. ← Multiply. ← Then subtract. Think: 3)12	$\begin{array}{r} 24 \\ 3\overline{)726} \\ -600 \\ \hline 126 \\ -120 \\ \hline 6 \\ - \\ \hline \end{array}$ ← Divide ones. ← Multiply. ← Subtract.

2 78 ÷ 6   6)78   **3** 63 ÷ 3   3)63   **4** 54 ÷ 2   2)54

5 378 ÷ 6   6)378   **6** 489 ÷ 3   3)489   **7** 543 ÷ 3   3)543

8 1,782 ÷ 6   6)1,782   **9** 8,091 ÷ 5   5)8,091   **10** 5,476 ÷ 2   2)5,476

☆   **Tell how you can use multiplication to check your answer.**

Divide. Show your work.

1 724 ÷ 6 = _____

2 335 ÷ 5 = _____

3 8,982 ÷ 2 = _____

4 162 ÷ 6 = _____

5 367 ÷ 3 = _____

6 623 ÷ 7 = _____

7 129 ÷ 6 = _____

8 4,623 ÷ 3 = _____

9 1,621 ÷ 4 = _____

10 427 ÷ 3 = _____

11 126 ÷ 5 = _____

12 771 ÷ 3 = _____

13 815 ÷ 5 = _____

14 616 ÷ 4 = _____

15 914 ÷ 8 = _____

16 413 ÷ 7 = _____

17 913 ÷ 9 = _____

18 754 ÷ 3 = _____

19 733 ÷ 9 = _____

20 828 ÷ 7 = _____

21 5,633 ÷ 6 = _____

22 4,415 ÷ 5 = _____

23 8,741 ÷ 6 = _____

24 3,798 ÷ 3 = _____

 Tell the steps you took to find the quotient.

 49

Name _____

Solve.

1 Our school has 6 grades and 786 students. What is the average number of students in each grade?

2 We have 72 eggs. Each container holds a half dozen. How many containers do we need for the eggs?

3 The area of the driveway is 384 square meters. The width of driveway is 4 meters. What is the length?

4 The dairy truck delivered 2,560 pints of whipping cream this week. If there are 8 pints in a gallon, how many gallons of whipping cream did the truck deliver?

5 The bus travels the same exact route each week, making 9 round trips from terminal Springfield to Burlington. If the bus travels 3,105 miles each week, how long is the bus route?

6 The movie theater collected $5,274 in ticket sales on Tuesday. If each ticket cost $9.00, how many tickets did they sell?

Circle the letter for the correct answer.

7 The jeweler needs 7 inches of gold chain to make a bracelet. If the jeweler has 750 inches of chain, how many bracelets can she make?

a) 108

b) 107

c) 106

d) 100

8 What is the quotient of 2,304 divided by 8?

a) 290

b) 388

c) 288

d) 278

Unit 10
Divide by a Two-Digit Divisor

Standard

Number & Operations in Base Ten
Perform operations with multi-digit whole numbers and with decimals to hundredths.
5.NBT.6 Find whole-number quotients of whole numbers with up to four-digit
        dividends and two-digit divisors, using strategies based on place
        value, the properties of operations, and/or the relationship between
        multiplication and division. Illustrate and explain the calculation by
        using equations, rectangular arrays, and/or area models.

Model the Skill

◆   Write the following division problem on the board with the corresponding model.

    $48 \div 12$

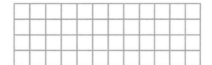

◆   **Ask:** *What is the quotient of 48 divided by 12?* (4)

◆   **Ask:** *How did you find the answer? What basic facts did you think about to help solve this problem?* (4 ÷ 1 and 8 ÷ 2) *How did you check your answer?* (multiply 12 by 4)

◆   Assign students the appropriate practice page(s) to support their understanding of the skill.

Assess the Skill

Use the following problems to pre-/post-assess students' understanding of the skill.

$980 \div 17$	$3{,}672 \div 18$	$8{,}030 \div 40$
$670 \div 62$	$4{,}543 \div 15$	$5{,}067 \div 29$

Name _____

Find the quotient for each problem.

1 189 ÷ 21

$$21 \overline{)189}$$ ← Look at tens.
21 > 18
There are no tens
or hundreds in the
quotient.

Decide where to place the first digit.

$$21 \overline{)189} \quad \begin{matrix} 9 \end{matrix}$$ ← Divide.
$$- \ 189$$ ← Multiply.
← Subtract.

---

2 46 ÷ 23 $$23 \overline{)46}$$

3 600 ÷ 24 $$24 \overline{)600}$$

---

4 99 ÷ 33 $$33 \overline{)99}$$

5 855 ÷ 45 $$45 \overline{)855}$$

---

6 840 ÷ 21 $$21 \overline{)840}$$

7 9,476 ÷ 46 $$46 \overline{)9,476}$$

☆ **Tell how you can use basic facts to find the quotient.**

Divide. Show your work.

1

$435 \div 15 =$ _____

$$15\overline{)435}$$
$$\overset{2}{}$$
$$-\ 300$$

2

$528 \div 88 =$ _____

$$88\overline{)528}$$

3

$726 \div 33 =$ _____

$$33\overline{)726}$$

4

$120 \div 15 =$ _____

$$15\overline{)120}$$

5

$968 \div 44 =$ _____

$$44\overline{)968}$$

6

$325 \div 13 =$ _____

$$13\overline{)325}$$

7

$9,605 \div 85 =$ _____

$$85\overline{)9,605}$$

8

$952 \div 56 =$ _____

$$56\overline{)952}$$

9

$720 \div 24 =$ _____

$$24\overline{)720}$$

10

$3,424 \div 16 =$ _____

$$16\overline{)3,424}$$

11

$3,692 \div 52 =$ _____

$$52\overline{)3,692}$$

12

$705 \div 47 =$ _____

$$47\overline{)705}$$

13

$2,660 \div 38 =$ _____

$$38\overline{)2,660}$$

14

$807 \div 30 =$ _____

$$30\overline{)807}$$

15

$6,902 \div 43 =$ _____

$$43\overline{)6,902}$$

16

$713 \div 20 =$ _____

$$20\overline{)713}$$

 Tell how you can use multiplication to check your answer.

Name _____

Divide. Show your work.

1 8,775 ÷ 45 = _____

2 3,006 ÷ 30 = _____

3 1,037 ÷ 61 = _____

4 9,058 ÷ 14 = _____

5 2,072 ÷ 56 = _____

6 4,005 ÷ 45 = _____

7 1,872 ÷ 24 = _____

8 1,675 ÷ 67 = _____

9 9,020 ÷ 22 = _____

10 4,472 ÷ 52 = _____

11 759 ÷ 23 = _____

12 8,075 ÷ 19 = _____

13 9,476 ÷ 46 = _____

14 8,833 ÷ 44 = _____

15 5,520 ÷ 23 = _____

16 8,575 ÷ 35 = _____

17 6,076 ÷ 56 = _____

18 894 ÷ 24 = _____

19 5,753 ÷ 11 = _____

20 3,990 ÷ 42 = _____

21 10,653 ÷ 53 = _____

22 9,943 ÷ 61 = _____

23 3,537 ÷ 27 = _____

24 6,080 ÷ 4 = _____

 Tell about what strategies you used to find the quotient.

Solve.

1 The theater has 352 seats. If there are 22 equal rows of seats, how many seats are in each row?

2 The perimeter of the bathroom is 372 inches. If there are 12 inches in a foot, what is the perimeter of the bathroom in feet?

3 If a space shuttle is traveling at 17,460 miles per hour, how fast is it moving per minute?

4 The area of the gym floor is 6,536 square feet. The length of the floor is 76 feet. What is the width?

5 The orchard sold 7,440 ounces of cherries last month. If there are 16 ounces in a pound, how many pounds of cherries did they sell?

6 The lumberyard sold 4,480 cubic feet of wood last week. If they sold 35 cords of wood in all, how many cubic feet is in a cord?

Circle the letter for the correct answer.

7 Last summer, we drove cross-country. The road trip was a total of 6,765 miles. If we go the same distance each day for 33 days, what was the average number of miles we drove each day?

a) 25

b) 250

c) 205

d) 215

8 Priscilla earned 781 dollars babysitting last year. If she charges $11 per hour, how many hours did she babysit?

a) 78

b) 77

c) 76

d) 71

Unit 11
Add and Subtract Decimals

Standard

Number & Operations in Base Ten
Perform operations with multi-digit whole numbers and with decimals to hundredths.
5.NBT.7 Add, subtract, multiply, and divide decimals to hundredths, using concrete models or drawings and strategies based on place value, properties of operations, and/or the relationship between addition and subtraction; relate the strategy to a written method and explain the reasoning used.

Model the Skill

◆ Write the following problem on the board.

$$0.6 + 0.12 \qquad \begin{array}{r} 0.6 \\ + \ 0.12 \\ \hline \end{array}$$

◆ Display a hundreds flat. **Say:** *Today we are going to see this as one whole. If this is one, what is a tens rod?* (one-tenth) *What is a ones cube?* (one-hundredth) *What is the sum of six-tenths and twelve-hundredths?* (seven-tenths and two-hundredths).

◆ Point to the vertical addition. **Ask:** *How do you add whole numbers?* (Add the columns starting on the right.) Guide students to add the decimals, starting with the hundredths place and regrouping as needed. **Say:** *The decimal points are lined up. Write a decimal point in the same position in the sum.* (0.72)

◆ Assign students the appropriate practice page(s) to support their understanding of the skill.

Assess the Skill

Use the following problems to pre-/post-assess students' understanding of the skill.

0.23 + 0.77	0.3 + 0.67	0.33 – 0.13	0.85 – 0.1
0.4 + 1.2	0.47 + 1.3	2.4 – 1.2	2.36 – 1.28

Solve. Use models or draw a picture.

❶ 0.35 + 0.26   0.35
                    + 0.26

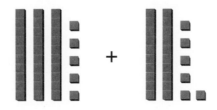

❷ 0.52 + 0.9   0.52
                   + 0.90

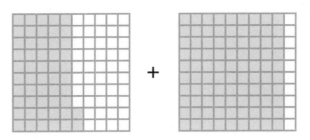

❸ 0.23 + 0.69   0.23
                   + 0.69

❹ 0.61 + 0.49   0.61
                   + 0.49

❺ 0.73 – 0.3   0.73
                   – 0.3

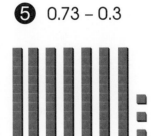

❻ 0.98 – 0.89   0.98
                   – 0.89

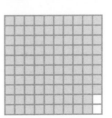

 Tell how you can use models to add decimals.

Name _____

Solve.

1

tens	ones	.	tenths	hundredths
	0	.	5	6
+	0	.	3	2

0.56 + 0.32   0.56
                   + 0.32

2

tens	ones	.	tenths	hundredths
	0	.	9	0
−	0	.	1	1

0.9 – 0.11   0.90
                  – 0.11

3

5.07 + 3.7   5.07
                  + 3.7

4

0.8 + 0.22   0.80
                  + 0.22

5

5.9 – 5.1   5.9
                 – 5.1

6

1.77 – 0.65   1.77
                   – 0.65

7

0.78 + 0.27   0.78
                   + 0.27

8

0.41 + 0.87   0.41
                   + 0.87

9

0.28 – 0.14   0.28
                   – 0.14

10

0.68 – 0.09   0.68
                   – 0.09

11

1.98 + 1.9   1.98
                  + 1.90

12

3.52 – 0.61   3.52
                   – 0.61

13

2.98 – 0.69   2.98
                   – 0.69

14

9.38 – 0.93   9.38
                   – 0.93

 Tell how you can use a place value chart to add decimals.

●●○

Solve.

1
1.7 + 0.38 = _____

2
2.6 − 0.72 = _____

3
3.65 + 1.52 = _____

4
40.7 − 0.38 = _____

5
15.06 + 10.5 = _____

6
5.06 − 1.9 = _____

7
7.8 − 4.08 = _____

8
20.6 + 20.01 = _____

9
4.33 − 0.43 = _____

10
17.3 − 3.4 = _____

11
6.02 + 0.89 = _____

12
6.33 + 0.63 = _____

13
9.8 − 2.12 = _____

14
9.08 + 3.62 = _____

15
4.03 − 3.37 = _____

16
1.56 + 1.64 = _____

17
5.36 + 1.44 = _____

18
10.1 + 1.01 = _____

19
7.6 − 0.93 = _____

20
2.85 − 0.81 = _____

21
4.93 + 4.62 = _____

22
12.8 + 0.02 = _____

23
3.8 − 3.42 = _____

24
508.1 − 37.61 = _____

 Tell how you can use addition to check your subtraction.

Name _____

Solve.

1 What is the sum of 7.8 and 7.02?

2 What is the difference between 13.04 and 12.06?

3 Sara bought a loaf of bread for $3.49 and a gallon of milk for $4.50. How much more did the milk cost?

4 Jamal put $0.75 in the parking meter. An hour later, he added another $0.50. How much did he put in the meter in all?

5 The salmon weighs 8.5 pounds. The mackerel weighs 6.62 pounds. How much do the two fish weigh in all?

6 Keith jumps 7.25 feet on the standing long jump. Tanya jumps 6.62 feet. How much farther can Keith jump?

Circle the letter for the correct answer.

7 The race is 10 kilometers. Tom has run 7.43 kilometers so far. How much farther does he need to run in order to finish the race?

a) 2.57 km

b) 2.67 km

c) 3.57 km

d) 3.67 km

8 The first song in the dance routine is 1.75 minutes long. The second song is 2.5 minutes. What is the combined time of both songs?

a) 2.0 minutes

b) 3.8 minutes

c) 3.25 minutes

d) 4.25 minutes

Unit 12
Multiply Decimals

Standard

Number & Operations in Base Ten
Perform operations with multi-digit whole numbers and with decimals to hundredths.
5.NBT.7 Add, subtract, multiply, and divide decimals to hundredths, using concrete models or drawings and strategies based on place value, properties of operations, and/or the relationship between addition and subtraction; relate the strategy to a written method and explain the reasoning used.

Model the Skill

◆ Write the following problem on the board.

$0.5 \times 0.9 =$

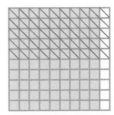

◆ **Say:** *Today we are going to multiply decimals using a hundredths grid to model the multiplication. The grid shows one whole. What does each row show?* (one-tenth) *What does each column show?* (one-tenth) *What two decimals are we multiplying in the problem?* (0.5 and 0.9) Guide students to see how each factor is shown on the grid. **Ask:** *How many squares are shaded by both factors?* (45) *What decimal names those squares?* (0.45) *What is five-tenths of nine-tenths?* (forty-five hundredths)

◆ Assign students the appropriate practice page(s) to support their understanding of the skill.

Assess the Skill

Use the following problems to pre-/post-assess students' understanding of the skill.

0.2×0.7	0.3×0.07	0.3×0.13	0.85×0.1
0.4×1.2	0.7×1.3	2.4×1.2	2.06×1.24

Name _____

Find each product. Use the grid to help.

Remember: The number of decimal places in the product is equal to the total number of decimal places in the factors.

❶

0.4 x 0.5 = _____

$$\begin{array}{r} 0.4 \\ \times\ 0.5 \\ \hline \end{array}$$

← 1 decimal place
← 1 decimal place
← Product has 2 decimal places.

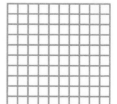

❷

0.51 x 7 = _____

$$\begin{array}{r} 0.51 \\ \times\ \ \ \ 7 \\ \hline \end{array}$$

← 2 decimal places
← 0 decimal places
← Product has 2 decimal places.

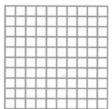

❸

0.9 x 0.2 = _____

$$\begin{array}{r} 0.9 \\ \times\ \ 0.2 \\ \hline \end{array}$$

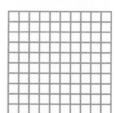

❹

0.7 x 0.3 = _____

$$\begin{array}{r} 0.7 \\ \times\ 0.3 \\ \hline \end{array}$$

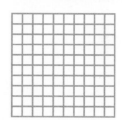

❺

1.81 x 0.5 = _____

$$\begin{array}{r} 1.81 \\ \times\ \ \ 0.5 \\ \hline \end{array}$$

❻

3.2 x 0.75 = _____

$$\begin{array}{r} 3.2 \\ \times\ 0.75 \\ \hline \end{array}$$

 Tell how you can use models to multiply decimals.

Find each product. Multiply as you would with whole numbers.

1 2.3 x 0.7

$$\begin{array}{r} \overset{2}{2.3} \leftarrow \text{1 decimal place} \\ \underline{\times\ 0.7} \leftarrow \text{1 decimal place} \\ 1.61 \leftarrow \text{Write the decimal} \end{array}$$
point in the product.

2 1.5 x 0.3

$$\begin{array}{r} 1.5 \\ \underline{\times\ 0.3} \end{array}$$

3 1.8 x 0.6

$$\begin{array}{r} 1.8 \\ \underline{\times\ 0.6} \end{array}$$

4 0.21 x 0.4

$$\begin{array}{r} 0.21 \\ \underline{\times\ 0.4} \end{array}$$

5 6.5 x 1.2

$$\begin{array}{r} 6.5 \\ \underline{\times\ 1.2} \end{array}$$

6 3.02 x 0.02

$$\begin{array}{r} 3.02 \\ \underline{\times\ 0.02} \end{array}$$

7 4.5 x 1.1

$$\begin{array}{r} 4.5 \\ \underline{\times\ 1.1} \end{array}$$

8 0.19 x 1.9

$$\begin{array}{r} 0.19 \\ \underline{\times\ 1.9} \end{array}$$

9 0.22 x 0.5

$$\begin{array}{r} 0.22 \\ \underline{\times\ 0.5} \end{array}$$

10 1.6 x 3.7

$$\begin{array}{r} 1.6 \\ \underline{\times\ 3.7} \end{array}$$

11 8.09 x 0.1

$$\begin{array}{r} 8.09 \\ \underline{\times\ 0.1} \end{array}$$

12 7.11 x 9.5

$$\begin{array}{r} 7.11 \\ \underline{\times\ 9.5} \end{array}$$

13 0.06 x 0.6

$$\begin{array}{r} 0.06 \\ \underline{\times\ 0.6} \end{array}$$

14 4.03 x 0.5

$$\begin{array}{r} 4.03 \\ \underline{\times\ 0.5} \end{array}$$

15 0.75 x 0.8

$$\begin{array}{r} 0.75 \\ \underline{\times\ 0.8} \end{array}$$

16 1.38 x 0.08

$$\begin{array}{r} 1.38 \\ \underline{\times\ 0.08} \end{array}$$

Name _____

Find each product. Multiply as you would with whole numbers.

1   0.5
      x   3

2   2.6
      x 0.8

3   4.39
      x 2.7

4   6.28
      x 0.02

5   4.5
      x 0.2

6   1.8
      x 0.5

7   10.73
      x   1.1

8   7.08
      x 0.02

9   3.2
      x 0.6

10   1.09
      x 0.3

11   1.7
      x 0.23

12   0.99
      x 0.11

13   5.5
      x 0.3

14   2.6
      x 0.8

15   10.09
      x   0.4

16   4.15
      x 0.03

17   8.31
      x   6

18   11.1
      x 0.9

19   2.08
      x 0.03

20   59.3
      x 0.07

21   40.5
      x 0.4

22 100.1
      x 0.7

23   4.7
      x 8.6

24   20.08
      x   0.09

☆   **Tell how you found the product.**

Name _____

Solve.

1 What is the product of 1.1 and 3.03?

2 What is the product of 10.04 and 2.8?

3 Harley bought some fabric for $3.50 per yard. If she bought 3 yards, how much did the fabric cost?

4 One can of corn is $1.09. If Mr. Ortiz buys 4 cans of corn, how much will it cost?

5 Jillian's favorite song is 1.5 minutes long. If she plays the song 5 times in a row, how long will she be listening to the song?

6 Charlie is making pancakes. The recipe says that he will need 1.75 cups of milk. If he doubles the recipe, how many cups of milk will he need?

Circle the letter for the correct answer.

7 Mrs. Pepe buys 0.5 pound of American cheese at the deli. If the price of American cheese is $6.50 per pound, how much does she pay for the cheese?

a) $32.50

b) $3.25

c) $0.325

d) $35.20

8 If the price of salmon is $9.99 per pound, how much does a 1.5-pound piece of salmon cost?

a) $14.99

b) $14.45

c) $12.45

d) $149.85

Unit 13
Divide Decimals

Standard

Number & Operations in Base Ten
Perform operations with multi-digit whole numbers and with decimals to hundredths.
5.NBT.7 Add, subtract, multiply, and divide decimals to hundredths, using concrete models or drawings and strategies based on place value, properties of operations, and/or the relationship between addition and subtraction; relate the strategy to a written method and explain the reasoning used.

Model the Skill

◆ **Say:** *Today we are going to divide decimals using base-ten blocks.* Hold up a hundreds flat and explain that it will represent one whole. **Ask:** *What is a base-ten block?* (one-tenth) *What is a ones cube?* (one-hundredth)

◆ Write the following problem on the board.

$5.4 \div 2 =$

◆ **Ask:** *How can you divide 5.4 into two groups?* (Possible answer: Put two wholes into each group; regroup 1 whole as 10 tenths and divide the 14 tenths into two groups of 7 tenths.) *What is 5.4 divided by 2?* (2.7)

◆ Direct students to another problem. **Ask:** *How can you divide 2.5 into 5 groups?* (Possible answer: Regroup each whole as 10 tenths so that there are 25 tenths. Then divide the 25 tenths into 5 groups with 5 each.) *What is 2.5 divided by 5?* (0.5)

◆ Assign students the appropriate practice page(s) to support their understanding of the skill.

Assess the Skill

Use the following problems to pre-/post-assess students' understanding of the skill.

$7.2 \div 2$	$0.35 \div 0.7$	$0.3 \div 0.6$	$1.85 \div 0.05$
$1.8 \div 3$	$7.5 \div 1.5$	$9.6 \div 1.2$	$2.06 \div 1.24$

Find each quotient. Use models to help.

1

0.8 ÷ 2 = _____

$$2\overline{)0.8}$$.

← Place the decimal point in the quotient directly above the decimal point in the dividend.

$$2\overline{)0.8}$$ 0.

2 1.5 ÷ 5 = _____

$$5\overline{)1.5}$$

3 6.12 ÷ 4 = _____

$$4\overline{)6.12}$$

4 4.02 ÷ 0.3 = _____

$$0.3\overline{)4.02}$$

Think:
$$4\overline{)32}$$

5 3.2 ÷ 0.4 = _____

$$0.4\overline{)3.2}$$

← Change the divisor to a whole number by multiplying the divisor by a power of 10. Then multiply the dividend by the same power of 10.

6 0.264 ÷ 0.06 = _____

$$0.06\overline{)0.264}$$

 Circle the quotient that shows hundredths.

Name _____

Find each quotient. Divide as you would with whole numbers.

1 8.06 ÷ 0.2 = _____

$0.2\overline{)8.06}$ ← Multiply the divisor and the dividend by 10.	$2\overline{)80.6}^{\ 4\ .}$ ← Place the decimal point in the quotient. ← Divide. _____ ← Multiply. ← Subtract. Think: $2\overline{)8}$	$2\overline{)8.06}^{\ 4.0}$ ← Bring down. Divide. $-8\ ↓$ _____ $0\ 0↓$ 6 Think: $2\overline{)0}=0$ and $0 \times 2 = 0.$ Write 0 in the quotient. Divide.

2 4.05 ÷ 5 = _____

$5\overline{)4.05}$

3 7.2 ÷ 0.9 = _____

$0.9\overline{)7.2}$

4 8.32 ÷ 0.8 = _____

$0.8\overline{)8.32}$

5 10.2 ÷ 0.2 = _____

$0.2\overline{)10.2}$

6 5.2 ÷ 5 = _____

$5\overline{)5.2}$

7 6.3 ÷ 0.3 = _____

$0.3\overline{)6.3}$

8 2.07 ÷ 3 = _____

$3\overline{)2.07}$

9 7.8 ÷ 0.4 = _____

$0.4\overline{)7.8}$

10 2.34 ÷ 0.03 = _____

$0.03\overline{)2.34}$

11 7.3 ÷ 0.2 = _____

$0.2\overline{)7.3}$

12 0.9 ÷ 3 = _____

$3\overline{)0.9}$

13 2.7 ÷ 0.09 = _____

$0.09\overline{)2.7}$

14 10.50 ÷ 0.5 = _____

$0.5\overline{)10.50}$

15 1.48 ÷ 0.3 = _____

$0.3\overline{)1.48}$

16 0.02 ÷ 2 = _____

$2\overline{)0.02}$

☆ **Tell how you can use multiplication to check your answer.**

Find each quotient. Divide as you would with whole numbers.

❶

$1.8 \div 5 =$ _____

$5\overline{)1.8}$

❷

$36 \div 1.2 =$ _____

$1.2\overline{)36}$

❸

$4.9 \div 0.7 =$ _____

$0.7\overline{)4.9}$

❹

$5.42 \div 0.8 =$ _____

$0.8\overline{)5.42}$

❺

$2.5 \div 50 =$ _____

❻

$17.2 \div 0.2 =$ _____

❼

$21.7 \div 3.5 =$ _____

❽

$17.5 \div 0.25 =$ _____

❾

$98 \div 25 =$ _____

❿

$36.75 \div 3 =$ _____

⓫

$4.05 \div 0.5 =$ _____

⓬

$23.31 \div 6.3 =$ _____

⓭

$1.17 \div 0.2 =$ _____

⓮

$4.5 \div 1.8 =$ _____

⓯

$5.8 \div 4 =$ _____

⓰

$3.2 \div 16 =$ _____

⓱

$371 \div 10.6 =$ _____

⓲

$74.2 \div 4 =$ _____

⓳

$3.3 \div 0.08 =$ _____

⓴

$59.25 \div 0.75 =$ _____

㉑

$4.5 \div 3 =$ _____

㉒

$41.6 \div 6.5 =$ _____

㉓

$101.1 \div 0.2 =$ _____

㉔

$9.9 \div 1.5 =$ _____

 Tell how you know your answer is correct.

Name _____

Find each quotient.

1 What is the quotient of 6.16 divided by 1.1?

2 What is the quotient of 12.75 divided by 3?

---

3 Heidi bought a set of eight plates at the antique store. She paid $77.20. How much did each plate cost?

4 Caleb spent $34.95 on 5 pounds of coffee. How much was the coffee per pound?

---

5 Michael returned a bag of cans and received $4.65 back. If the deposit for each can was $0.05, how many cans did he return?

6 Olivia bought 3 containers of orange juice. She bought a total of 90.6 ounces of juice. How many ounces are in each container?

Circle the letter for the correct answer.

7 Frederick paid $45.96 for 4 beach towels. How much did each beach towel cost?

a) $11.29

b) $11.39

c) $11.49

d) $9.99

8 Maggie paid $47.25 for 3.5 kilograms of shrimp. What is the price of shrimp per kilogram?

a) $13.50

b) $13.00

c) $12.50

d) $13.75

Unit 14
Add Fractions

Standard

Number & Operations—Fractions
Use equivalent fractions as a strategy to add and subtract fractions.
5.NF.1 Add and subtract fractions with unlike denominators (including mixed numbers) by replacing given fractions with equivalent fractions in such a way as to produce an equivalent sum or difference of fractions with like denominators.
5.NF.2 Solve word problems involving addition and subtraction of fractions referring to the same whole, including cases of unlike denominators. Use benchmark fractions and number sense of fractions to estimate mentally and assess the reasonableness of answers.

Model the Skill

◆ **Say:** *Today we are going to add fractions.* Write $\frac{1}{5} + \frac{2}{5}$ on the board. **Ask:** *How do we add fractions that have the same denominator?* (add the numerators) Have students look at the problem and discuss how they might add the fractions when the denominators are different.

◆ Write $\frac{1}{3} + \frac{1}{6}$ on the board. **Ask:** *What can we do to write these fractions with a common denominator—denominators that are the same? How can we use equivalent fractions?* Help students understand that when one denominator is a multiple of the other denominator, they can simply write an equivalent fraction. Review how to find equivalent fractions by multiplying ($\frac{1}{3}$ x $\frac{2}{2}$ = $\frac{2}{6}$) or dividing.

◆ Assign students the appropriate practice page(s) to support their understanding of the skill.

Assess the Skill

Use the following problems to pre-/post-assess students' understanding of the skill.

$\frac{1}{2} + \frac{1}{2}$ $\qquad$ $\frac{1}{3} + \frac{2}{3}$ $\qquad$ $\frac{1}{4} + \frac{1}{4}$ $\qquad$ $\frac{3}{5} + \frac{1}{5}$

$\frac{1}{2} + \frac{2}{3}$ $\qquad$ $\frac{4}{5} + \frac{1}{4}$ $\qquad$ $\frac{5}{6} + \frac{1}{3}$ $\qquad$ $\frac{5}{7} + \frac{2}{5}$

Name _____

Write an equivalent fraction. Then find the sum.

❶

$\dfrac{1}{6}$ + $\dfrac{1}{2}$

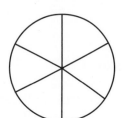

❷

$\dfrac{1}{8}$ + $\dfrac{3}{4}$

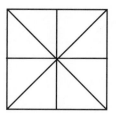

❸

$\dfrac{1}{3}$ + $\dfrac{3}{6}$

❹

$\dfrac{1}{4}$ + $\dfrac{3}{8}$

❺

$\dfrac{1}{2}$ + $\dfrac{5}{6}$

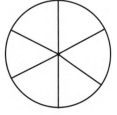

❻

$\dfrac{1}{3}$ + $\dfrac{4}{9}$

 Tell how you add fractions.

Name _____

Find a common denominator. Add.

1 $\frac{1}{3}$ + $\frac{1}{2}$ $\frac{1}{2}$ × $\frac{3}{3}$ + $\frac{1}{3}$ × $\frac{2}{2}$ = $\frac{3}{6}$ + $\frac{2}{6}$ =   —

2 $\frac{1}{4}$ + $\frac{1}{2}$ $\frac{1}{4}$ + $\frac{1}{2}$ × $\frac{2}{2}$ = $\frac{1}{4}$ + $\frac{2}{4}$ =   —

3 $\frac{3}{4}$ + $\frac{1}{2}$

4 $\frac{5}{6}$ + $\frac{1}{2}$

5 $\frac{3}{6}$ + $\frac{1}{2}$

6 $\frac{1}{6}$ + $\frac{4}{8}$

7 $\frac{7}{8}$ + $\frac{1}{4}$

8 $\frac{3}{8}$ + $\frac{1}{2}$

 Tell how you find the common denominator.

Name _____

Find each sum. Use symbols to tell if the sum is greater than (>) or less than (<) 1.

1 $\dfrac{1}{3} + \dfrac{1}{6}$ **2** $\dfrac{3}{4} + \dfrac{1}{2}$ **3** $\dfrac{3}{5} + \dfrac{1}{10}$ **4** $\dfrac{1}{4} + \dfrac{3}{8}$

5 $\dfrac{2}{3} + \dfrac{1}{9}$ **6** $\dfrac{1}{5} + \dfrac{7}{10}$ **7** $\dfrac{1}{8} + \dfrac{1}{2}$ **8** $\dfrac{3}{4} + \dfrac{5}{8}$

9 $\dfrac{5}{7} + \dfrac{1}{5}$ **10** $\dfrac{1}{3} + \dfrac{7}{12}$ **11** $\dfrac{2}{3} + \dfrac{1}{5}$ **12** $\dfrac{1}{6} + \dfrac{6}{9}$

13 $\dfrac{3}{10} + \dfrac{4}{5}$ **14** $\dfrac{1}{8} + \dfrac{5}{12}$ **15** $\dfrac{1}{3} + \dfrac{4}{7}$ **16** $\dfrac{7}{8} + \dfrac{1}{10}$

☆ **Tell how you know if the sum will be greater than 1.**

Name _____

Solve.

1 What is the sum of $\frac{1}{8}$ and $\frac{3}{4}$?

2 What is the sum of $\frac{2}{5}$ and $\frac{1}{4}$?

3 What is the sum of $\frac{3}{5}$ and $\frac{3}{7}$?

4 The chapter is 8 pages long. Kosta read $\frac{1}{4}$ of the chapter aloud. Then Christina read three pages to the class. How many pages have they read so far?

5 Clara ate $\frac{1}{8}$ of the pie. Jacob ate $\frac{1}{4}$. How much of the pie did they eat in all?

6 The tangerine had 12 sections. I ate five sections. Dad ate $\frac{1}{3}$. How much of the tangerine did we eat?

Circle the letter for the correct answer.

7 The inn has ten rooms. One-half of the rooms are reserved for Friday. The rest are vacant. If 2 more rooms are reserved for Friday, what will be the total number of occupied rooms on Friday?

a) $\frac{5}{12}$

b) $\frac{5}{10}$

c) $\frac{7}{8}$

d) $\frac{7}{10}$

8 What is the sum of seven-eighths and one-sixteenth?

a) $\frac{15}{16}$

b) $\frac{14}{16}$

c) $\frac{7}{8}$

d) $\frac{8}{16}$

Unit 15
Subtract Fractions

Number & Operations—Fractions
Use equivalent fractions as a strategy to add and subtract fractions.
5.NF.1 Add and subtract fractions with unlike denominators (including mixed numbers) by replacing given fractions with equivalent fractions in such a way as to produce an equivalent sum or difference of fractions with like denominators.
5.NF.2 Solve word problems involving addition and subtraction of fractions referring to the same whole, including cases of unlike denominators. Use benchmark fractions and number sense of fractions to estimate mentally and assess the reasonableness of answers.

Model the Skill

◆ **Say:** *Today we are going to subtract fractions. Write $\frac{2}{5} - \frac{1}{5}$ on the board.*
Ask: *How do we subtract fractions that have the same denominator?* (Subtract the numerators.)

◆ **Ask:** *What is the first thing we need to do to subtract fractions with unlike denominators?* (Use equivalent fractions to write common denominators.) Help students find an equivalent fraction for $\frac{1}{3}$ with a denominator of 6. ($\frac{2}{6}$) Review how to find equivalent fractions.

◆ Assign students the appropriate practice page(s) to support their understanding of the skill.

Assess the Skill

Use the following problems to pre-/post-assess students' understanding of the skill.

$$\frac{3}{4} - \frac{1}{2} \qquad \frac{2}{3} - \frac{1}{3} \qquad \frac{3}{4} - \frac{1}{5} \qquad \frac{3}{5} - \frac{1}{5}$$

$$\frac{2}{3} - \frac{1}{3} \qquad \frac{4}{5} - \frac{1}{4} \qquad \frac{5}{6} - \frac{1}{3} \qquad \frac{5}{7} - \frac{2}{5}$$

Name _____

Write an equivalent fraction. Then find the difference.

1

$\dfrac{3}{6}$ − $\dfrac{1}{3}$

2

$\dfrac{5}{8}$ − $\dfrac{1}{4}$

3

$\dfrac{2}{3}$ − $\dfrac{2}{6}$

4

$\dfrac{9}{10}$ − $\dfrac{2}{5}$

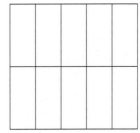

5

$\dfrac{1}{3}$ − $\dfrac{1}{9}$

6

$\dfrac{2}{3}$ − $\dfrac{3}{12}$

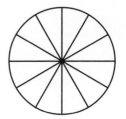

 Tell how you subtract fractions.

Name _____

Find a common denominator. Subtract.

1 $\dfrac{1}{2}$ – $\dfrac{1}{3}$ $\dfrac{1}{2}$ x $\dfrac{3}{3}$ – $\dfrac{1}{3}$ x $\dfrac{2}{2}$ = $\dfrac{3}{6}$ – $\dfrac{2}{6}$ = ___

2 $\dfrac{3}{4}$ – $\dfrac{1}{2}$ $\dfrac{3}{4}$ – $\dfrac{1}{2}$ x $\dfrac{2}{2}$ = $\dfrac{3}{4}$ – $\dfrac{2}{4}$ = ___

3 $\dfrac{4}{5}$ – $\dfrac{1}{2}$

4 $\dfrac{5}{6}$ – $\dfrac{1}{2}$

5 $\dfrac{3}{6}$ – $\dfrac{1}{2}$

6 $\dfrac{4}{6}$ – $\dfrac{4}{8}$

7 $\dfrac{7}{8}$ – $\dfrac{1}{4}$

8 $\dfrac{5}{8}$ – $\dfrac{1}{2}$

☆   **Tell how you found the common denominator.**

●●○

Name _____

Solve.

1 $\dfrac{1}{3} - \dfrac{1}{6}$ **2** $\dfrac{3}{4} - \dfrac{1}{2}$ **3** $\dfrac{3}{5} - \dfrac{1}{10}$ **4** $\dfrac{3}{4} - \dfrac{3}{8}$

5 $\dfrac{2}{3} - \dfrac{1}{9}$ **6** $\dfrac{1}{5} - \dfrac{2}{10}$ **7** $\dfrac{1}{2} - \dfrac{1}{8}$ **8** $\dfrac{3}{4} - \dfrac{5}{8}$

9 $\dfrac{5}{7} - \dfrac{1}{5}$ **10** $\dfrac{2}{3} - \dfrac{5}{12}$ **11** $\dfrac{2}{3} - \dfrac{1}{5}$ **12** $\dfrac{6}{9} - \dfrac{3}{5}$

13 $\dfrac{9}{10} - \dfrac{3}{5}$ **14** $\dfrac{7}{8} - \dfrac{5}{12}$ **15** $\dfrac{1}{2} - \dfrac{2}{7}$ **16** $\dfrac{7}{8} - \dfrac{1}{10}$

 Tell how you could estimate the difference.

●●● 79

Name _____

Solve.

1 What is the difference between $\frac{3}{5}$ and $\frac{2}{10}$?

2 What is the difference between $\frac{3}{4}$ and $\frac{3}{10}$?

3 What is the difference between $\frac{4}{5}$ and $\frac{3}{8}$?

4 Kim has finished eight of the ten math problems. Phil has finished $\frac{2}{5}$ of the problems. How much more of the math has Kim finished?

5 Cynthia ate $\frac{1}{4}$ of the pizza. If the pizza has eight slices, how many slices are left?

6 The clementine had 12 sections. Noah ate $\frac{3}{4}$ of them. How many sections are left?

Circle the letter for the correct answer.

7 Bella grew $\frac{3}{4}$ of an inch last year. Ben grew $\frac{7}{10}$ of an inch. Who grew more?

  a) Bella grew $\frac{1}{20}$ of an inch more.

  b) Ben grew $\frac{1}{10}$ of an inch more.

  c) Bella grew $\frac{1}{10}$ of an inch more.

  d) Ben grew $\frac{1}{20}$ of an inch more.

8 What is the difference between three-twelfths and five-eighths?

  a) $\frac{1}{3}$

  b) $\frac{3}{8}$

  c) $\frac{11}{24}$

  d) $\frac{7}{8}$

Unit 16
Multiply Whole Numbers and Fractions

Standard

Number & Operations—Fractions
Apply and extend previous understandings of multiplication and division to multiply and divide fractions.
5.NF.3 Interpret a fraction as division of the numerator by the denominator ($a/b = a \div b$). Solve word problems involving division of whole numbers leading to answers in the form of fractions or mixed numbers.
5.NF.4 Apply and extend previous understandings of multiplication to multiply a fraction or whole number by a fraction.
5.NF.5 Interpret multiplication as scaling (resizing).

Model the Skill

◆ **Say:** *Today we are going to multiply a fraction and a whole number. When we multiply two whole numbers, like 3 x 6, will the product be more or less than 6?* (more) *If we multiply 6 by a fraction, will the product be more or less than 6?* (less) *Why?* Help students understand that when multiplying by a fraction, they are finding a part of the whole number.

◆ Write the following problem on the board.

$$\frac{1}{3} \times 6$$

◆ **Ask:** *Why does $\frac{1}{3}$ of 6 equal 2?* Build the idea of partitioning (dividing) into equal groups as a way to understand multiplying by a fraction.

◆ Assign students the appropriate practice page(s) to support their understanding of the skill.

Assess the Skill

Use the following problems to pre-/post-assess students' understanding of the skill.

$5 \times \dfrac{1}{2}$ $\dfrac{2}{3} \times 3$ $15 \times \dfrac{1}{5}$ $\dfrac{3}{5} \times 4$

$12 \times \dfrac{1}{3}$ $16 \times \dfrac{1}{4}$ $7 \times \dfrac{1}{3}$ $5 \times \dfrac{2}{5}$

Name _____

Find a fraction of a whole number.

1 $\frac{1}{2}$ of 6

$\frac{1}{2}$ × 6 = _____

2 $\frac{1}{3}$ of 6

$\frac{1}{3}$ × 6 = _____

3 $\frac{1}{4}$ of 12

$\frac{1}{4}$ × 12 = _____

4 $\frac{1}{2}$ of 10

$\frac{1}{2}$ × 10 = _____

5 $\frac{1}{4}$ of 8

$\frac{1}{4}$ × 8 = _____

6 $\frac{1}{3}$ of 12

$\frac{1}{3}$ × 12 = _____

☆ **Circle the problem with the greatest product.**

Multiply. Write each product as a whole number.

 ❶ $\frac{1}{3} \times 9 = \dfrac{\square}{\square} =$ _____

$\frac{1}{3}$ **of a set of 9**

$9 \times \frac{1}{3} = \dfrac{\square}{\square} =$ _____

9 sets of $\frac{1}{3}$

---

❷ $\frac{1}{2} \times 6$

$\frac{1}{2} \times \frac{6}{1} = \dfrac{\square}{\square} =$ _____

❸ $8 \times \frac{1}{4}$

$\frac{8}{1} \times \frac{1}{4} = \dfrac{\square}{\square} =$ _____

❹ $\frac{1}{6} \times 12$

$12 \times \frac{1}{6} = \dfrac{\square}{\square} =$ _____

---

❺ $\frac{2}{5} \times 10$

$\frac{2}{5} \times \frac{10}{1} = \dfrac{\square}{\square} =$ _____

❻ $6 \times \frac{2}{3}$

$\frac{6}{1} \times \frac{2}{3} = \dfrac{\square}{\square} =$ _____

❼ $\frac{5}{6} \times 12$

$12 \times \frac{5}{6} = \dfrac{\square}{\square} =$ _____

---

❽ $\frac{3}{4} \times 8$

$\frac{3}{4} \times \frac{8}{1} = \dfrac{\square}{\square} =$ _____

❾ $12 \times \frac{4}{5}$

$\frac{12}{1} \times \frac{4}{5} = \dfrac{\square}{\square} =$ _____

❿ $\frac{5}{7} \times 5$

$5 \times \frac{5}{7} = \dfrac{\square}{\square} =$ _____

   Tell how you simplified the product.

Name _____

Multiply. Write the answer in simplest form.

1 $\frac{2}{5}$ x 10

$\frac{2}{5}$ x $\frac{10}{\square}$ = $\frac{\square}{\square}$ = _____

2 $\frac{3}{6}$ x 8

$\frac{\square}{\square}$ x $\frac{\square}{\square}$ = $\frac{\square}{\square}$ = _____

3 $\frac{4}{5}$ x 9

$\frac{\square}{\square}$ x $\frac{\square}{\square}$ = $\frac{\square}{\square}$ = _____

4 $\frac{5}{6}$ x 10

$\frac{\square}{\square}$ x $\frac{\square}{\square}$ = $\frac{\square}{\square}$ = _____

5 $\frac{3}{4}$ x 6

$\frac{\square}{\square}$ x $\frac{\square}{\square}$ = $\frac{\square}{\square}$ = _____

6 $\frac{2}{3}$ x 9

$\frac{\square}{\square}$ x $\frac{\square}{\square}$ = $\frac{\square}{\square}$ = _____

7 $\frac{3}{4}$ x 8

$\frac{\square}{\square}$ x $\frac{\square}{\square}$ = $\frac{\square}{\square}$ = _____

8 $\frac{2}{5}$ x 12

$\frac{\square}{\square}$ x $\frac{\square}{\square}$ = $\frac{\square}{\square}$ = _____

9 $\frac{1}{4}$ x 16

$\frac{\square}{\square}$ x $\frac{\square}{\square}$ = $\frac{\square}{\square}$ = _____

10 $\frac{2}{5}$ x 7

$\frac{\square}{\square}$ x $\frac{\square}{\square}$ = $\frac{\square}{\square}$ = _____

11 $\frac{1}{3}$ x 14

$\frac{\square}{\square}$ x $\frac{\square}{\square}$ = $\frac{\square}{\square}$ = _____

12 $\frac{1}{2}$ x 11

$\frac{\square}{\square}$ x $\frac{\square}{\square}$ = $\frac{\square}{\square}$ = _____

13 $\frac{3}{10}$ x 7

$\frac{\square}{\square}$ x $\frac{\square}{\square}$ = $\frac{\square}{\square}$ = _____

14 $\frac{5}{8}$ x 4

$\frac{\square}{\square}$ x $\frac{\square}{\square}$ = $\frac{\square}{\square}$ = _____

15 $\frac{2}{6}$ x 18

$\frac{\square}{\square}$ x $\frac{\square}{\square}$ = $\frac{\square}{\square}$ = _____

16 $\frac{5}{7}$ x 10

$\frac{\square}{\square}$ x $\frac{\square}{\square}$ = $\frac{\square}{\square}$ = _____

☆ **Explain the steps you took to find the product.**

Solve each problem. Write the answer in simplest form. Show your work.

1 Jack bought a 16-pound bag of dog food. His dog ate $\frac{2}{3}$ of the food in a month. How many pounds of food did the dog eat in a month?

2 Abigail has a 12-ounce glass of milk. She drinks $\frac{3}{4}$ of the glass. How many ounces of milk did she drink?

3 Zoe has 3 square meters of fabric. She needs $\frac{5}{6}$ of the fabric to make a skirt. How much fabric will she use to make the skirt?

4 Ryan has 15 meters of stereo wire. He used $\frac{7}{8}$ of the wire to hook up his new speakers. How much wire did he use?

5 The post office sold 900 stamps yesterday. $\frac{1}{4}$ of the stamps were postcard stamps. How many postcard stamps did they sell?

6 The bakery sold 65 cheesecakes yesterday. $\frac{3}{5}$ of the cheesecakes were chocolate. How many chocolate cheesecakes did they sell?

Circle the letter for the correct answer.

7 What is the product of $\frac{7}{8}$ and 14?

a) $12\frac{3}{8}$

b) $9\frac{3}{4}$

c) 12

d) $12\frac{1}{4}$

8 The price of a hat is $27. When it goes on sale, it will be $\frac{1}{3}$ less. How much would you save if you were to buy it on sale?

a) $8

b) $9

c) $18

d) $19

Unit 17
Multiply Fractions

Standard

Number & Operations—Fractions
Apply and extend previous understandings of multiplication and division to multiply and divide fractions.
5.NF.3 Interpret a fraction as division of the numerator by the denominator ($a/b = a \div b$). Solve word problems involving division of whole numbers leading to answers in the form of fractions or mixed numbers.
5.NF.4 Apply and extend previous understandings of multiplication to multiply a fraction or whole number by a fraction.
5.NF.5 Interpret multiplication as scaling (resizing).

Model the Skill

◆ Write the following problem and corresponding model on the board.

$$\frac{2}{3} \times \frac{1}{2} = \underline{\hspace{1.5cm}}$$

$$\frac{1}{2} \times \frac{2}{3} = \underline{\hspace{1.5cm}}$$

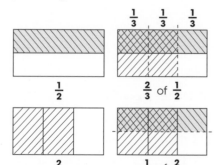

◆ **Say:** *When we multiplied two whole numbers, the product was greater than each factor. When we multiply two fractions, like $\frac{2}{3} \times \frac{1}{2}$, will the product be greater or less than each factor?* (less) *Why?* Help students understand that when multiplying two fractions, they are finding a fraction of a part.

◆ Have students look at the problem and explain what the art shows. **Ask:** *Why is the product $\frac{2}{6}$?* Have students identify $\frac{1}{2}$ of the whole and $\frac{2}{3}$ of the whole. Then have them point to the section that represents $\frac{2}{3}$ of $\frac{1}{2}$.

◆ **Say:** *Is the fraction $\frac{2}{6}$ in its simplest form?* (no) *How can you simplify $\frac{2}{6}$?* (divide by $\frac{2}{2}$ and reduce the fraction to $\frac{1}{3}$)

◆ Assign students the appropriate practice page(s) to support their understanding of the skill.

Assess the Skill

Use the following problems to pre-/post-assess students' understanding of the skill.

$$\frac{4}{5} \times \frac{1}{2} \qquad\qquad\qquad \frac{1}{3} \times \frac{3}{4}$$

Find a fraction of a part.

1 $\frac{1}{2}$ of $\frac{1}{3}$

$\frac{1}{2}$ x $\frac{1}{3}$ = _____

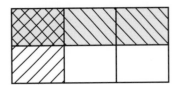

2 $\frac{1}{2}$ of $\frac{1}{4}$

$\frac{1}{2}$ x $\frac{1}{4}$ = _____

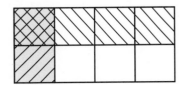

3 $\frac{1}{4}$ of $\frac{1}{3}$

$\frac{1}{4}$ x $\frac{1}{3}$ = _____

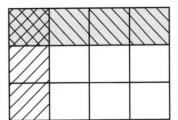

4 $\frac{4}{5}$ of $\frac{1}{2}$

$\frac{4}{5}$ x $\frac{1}{2}$ = _____

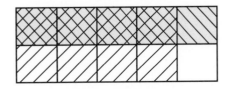

5 $\frac{1}{4}$ of $\frac{2}{3}$

$\frac{1}{4}$ x $\frac{2}{3}$ = _____

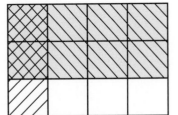

6 $\frac{1}{8}$ of $\frac{3}{4}$

$\frac{1}{8}$ x $\frac{3}{4}$ = _____

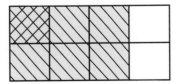

 Tell how you know the product will be less than one-half.

Name _____

Multiply. Show your work.

 1

$\frac{2}{3}$ x $\frac{1}{2}$ = _____

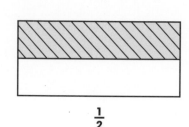

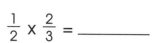

$\frac{1}{2}$ x $\frac{2}{3}$ = _____

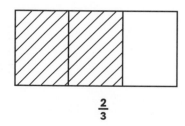

2

$\frac{5}{8}$ x $\frac{1}{2}$ = _____

3

$\frac{1}{4}$ x $\frac{4}{5}$ = _____

4

$\frac{3}{4}$ x $\frac{1}{2}$ = _____

5

$\frac{5}{6}$ x $\frac{3}{4}$ = _____

6

$\frac{1}{8}$ x $\frac{2}{5}$ = _____

7

$\frac{7}{8}$ x $\frac{2}{3}$ = _____

8

$\frac{1}{6}$ x $\frac{6}{7}$ = _____

9

$\frac{3}{4}$ x $\frac{2}{8}$ = _____

10

$\frac{5}{9}$ x $\frac{1}{6}$ = _____

 Tell how you multiplied the fractions.

Name _____

Multiply. Write the answer in simplest form.

1 $\frac{1}{3} \times \frac{2}{4} = \frac{\square}{\square} = $ ____

2 $\frac{2}{3} \times \frac{2}{3} = \frac{\square}{\square} = $ ____

3 $\frac{5}{8} \times \frac{1}{4} = \frac{\square}{\square} = $ ____

4 $\frac{1}{7} \times \frac{5}{6} = \frac{\square}{\square} = $ ____

5 $\frac{6}{8} \times \frac{1}{4} = \frac{\square}{\square} = $ ____

6 $\frac{2}{5} \times \frac{1}{3} = \frac{\square}{\square} = $ ____

7 $\frac{6}{8} \times \frac{3}{4} = \frac{\square}{\square} = $ ____

8 $\frac{1}{8} \times \frac{3}{5} = \frac{\square}{\square} = $ ____

9 $\frac{2}{6} \times \frac{1}{5} = \frac{\square}{\square} = $ ____

10 $\frac{3}{8} \times \frac{2}{3} = \frac{\square}{\square} = $ ____

11 $\frac{2}{9} \times \frac{3}{4} = \frac{\square}{\square} = $ ____

12 $\frac{5}{6} \times \frac{2}{3} = \frac{\square}{\square} = $ ____

13 $\frac{3}{5} \times \frac{5}{7} = \frac{\square}{\square} = $ ____

14 $\frac{4}{5} \times \frac{3}{8} = \frac{\square}{\square} = $ ____

15 $\frac{1}{5} \times \frac{4}{8} = \frac{\square}{\square} = $ ____

16 $\frac{3}{10} \times \frac{9}{10} = \frac{\square}{\square} = $ ____

 Tell how you found the simplest form of the product.

Name _____

Solve each problem. Write the answer in simplest form. Show your work.

1 Reiki has $\frac{3}{4}$ of a gallon of milk. She drinks one-third of the milk. How much milk does she drink?

2 Francesca bought $\frac{2}{3}$ of a pound of sliced turkey. She used half of the turkey to make sandwiches. How much turkey did she use?

3 Michael has to walk $\frac{3}{8}$ of a kilometer to the store. He walks $\frac{4}{5}$ of the way. How far did he walk?

4 Owen has $\frac{5}{6}$ of a yard of sailcloth. He uses $\frac{2}{3}$ of the cloth to recover a seat cushion. How much cloth does he use?

5 Nine-tenths of the students in the class completed their homework. Two-thirds of those students got the bonus question correct. What fraction of the class got the bonus question correct?

6 Three-fifths of the students voted for Kylie to become class president. Two-thirds of those students were girls. What fraction shows the number of girls in the class who voted for Kylie?

Circle the letter for the correct answer.

7 What is the product of $\frac{3}{7}$ and $\frac{5}{8}$?

a) 1

b) $\frac{1}{11}$

c) $\frac{15}{56}$

d) $\frac{1}{4}$

8 Two-thirds of the tables in the restaurant are taken. Six of those 10 tables haven't ordered their food yet. What fraction of the seated tables still have to order their food?

a) $\frac{6}{10}$

b) $\frac{8}{13}$

c) $\frac{2}{15}$

d) $\frac{2}{5}$

Unit 18
Multiply Mixed Numbers

Standard

Number & Operations—Fractions
Apply and extend previous understandings of multiplication and division to multiply and divide fractions.
5.NF.3 Interpret a fraction as division of the numerator by the denominator ($a/b = a \div b$). Solve word problems involving division of whole numbers leading to answers in the form of fractions or mixed numbers.
5.NF.4 Apply and extend previous understandings of multiplication to multiply a fraction or whole number by a fraction.
5.NF.5 Interpret multiplication as scaling (resizing).
5.NF.6 Solve real world problems involving multiplication of fractions and mixed numbers, e.g., by using visual fraction models or equations to represent the problem.
5.NF.7 Apply and extend previous understandings of division to divide unit fractions by whole numbers and whole numbers by unit fractions.

Model the Skill

◆ Write the following problem and corresponding model on the board.

$\frac{1}{4}$ x $1\frac{1}{2}$ = _____

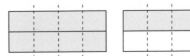

◆ **Say:** *Today we are going to multiply mixed numbers. We multiply mixed numbers the same way we multiply fractions. Look at the problem. How can we write $1\frac{1}{2}$ as a fraction?* ($\frac{2}{2} + \frac{1}{2} = \frac{3}{2}$) Have students use the art to explain the improper fraction.

◆ **Say:** *Now we are going to take $\frac{1}{4}$ of 3 halves, so we cut $1\frac{1}{2}$ into fourths.* Have students look at the art. **Ask:** *How many fourths should we mark with an X?* ($\frac{1}{4}$ of each rectangle) Have them count the number of parts in one whole rectangle. (8) The part that is both shaded and has an X is the product. Connect the algorithm to the art. ($\frac{1}{4}$ x $\frac{3}{2}$ = $\frac{3}{8}$)

◆ Assign students the appropriate practice page(s) to support their understanding of the skill.

Assess the Skill

Use the following problems to pre-/post-assess students' understanding of the skill.

$2\frac{1}{4}$ x $\frac{1}{3}$ $3\frac{1}{2}$ x $\frac{1}{3}$ $1\frac{3}{4}$ x $\frac{1}{3}$ $4\frac{1}{4}$ x $\frac{1}{5}$

$1\frac{3}{4}$ x $\frac{1}{2}$ $5\frac{1}{5}$ x $\frac{1}{2}$ $1\frac{2}{5}$ x $\frac{1}{2}$ $2\frac{5}{6}$ x $\frac{2}{5}$

Name _____

Write a mixed number as an improper fraction. Then multiply.

1 $\frac{1}{4}$ x $1\frac{1}{2}$

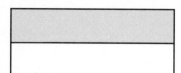

$1\frac{1}{2}$ = $\frac{\square}{2}$

$1\frac{1}{2}$ or $\frac{3}{2}$ shaded

$\frac{1}{4}$ x $\frac{\square}{2}$ = _____

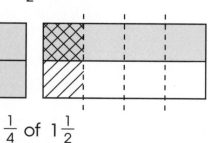

$\frac{1}{4}$ of $1\frac{1}{2}$

2 $\frac{1}{8}$ x $2\frac{1}{2}$

$2\frac{1}{2}$ = $\frac{\square}{2}$

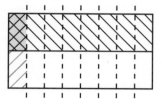

$\frac{1}{8}$ x $\frac{\square}{2}$ = _____

3 $2\frac{2}{3}$ x $\frac{1}{5}$

$2\frac{2}{3}$ = $\frac{\square}{3}$

$\frac{\square}{3}$ x $\frac{1}{5}$ = _____

4 $\frac{1}{3}$ x $1\frac{3}{4}$

$1\frac{3}{4}$ = $\frac{\square}{4}$

$\frac{1}{3}$ x $\frac{\square}{4}$ = _____

  Tell how you write a mixed number as an improper fraction.

Multiply. Write the answer in simplest form.

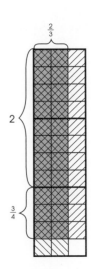

1

$2\frac{3}{4} \times \frac{2}{3}$

$2\frac{3}{4} = \frac{\square}{4}$

$\frac{\square}{4} \times \frac{2}{3} = $ _____

---

2 $1\frac{3}{5} \times \frac{5}{6}$

$1\frac{3}{5} = \frac{\square}{5}$

$\frac{\square}{5} \times \frac{5}{6} = $ _____

3 $2\frac{1}{4} \times \frac{1}{3}$

$2\frac{1}{4} = \frac{\square}{4}$

$\frac{\square}{4} \times \frac{1}{3} = $ _____

4 $3\frac{3}{8} \times \frac{1}{6}$

$3\frac{3}{8} = \frac{\square}{8}$

$\frac{\square}{8} \times \frac{1}{6} = $ _____

---

5 $\frac{5}{8} \times 5\frac{1}{4}$

$5\frac{1}{4} = \frac{\square}{4}$

$\frac{5}{8} \times \frac{\square}{4} = $ _____

6 $\frac{2}{7} \times 3\frac{2}{4}$

$3\frac{2}{4} = \frac{\square}{4}$

$\frac{2}{7} \times \frac{\square}{4} = $ _____

7 $\frac{1}{6} \times 4\frac{3}{4}$

$4\frac{3}{4} = \frac{\square}{4}$

$\frac{1}{6} \times \frac{\square}{4} = $ _____

---

8 $\frac{3}{10} \times 2\frac{2}{5}$

$2\frac{2}{5} = \frac{\square}{5}$

$\frac{3}{10} \times \frac{\square}{5} = $ _____

9 $\frac{4}{5} \times 2\frac{1}{8}$

$2\frac{1}{8} = \frac{\square}{8}$

$\frac{4}{5} \times \frac{\square}{8} = $ _____

10 $\frac{4}{5} \times 10\frac{1}{6}$

$10\frac{1}{6} = \frac{\square}{6}$

$\frac{4}{5} \times \frac{\square}{6} = $ _____

  Tell how you find the simplest form of a fraction.

Name _____

Multiply. Write the answer in simplest form.

1 $1\frac{1}{2} \times 2\frac{1}{2}$

$\frac{\square}{2} \times \frac{\square}{2} =$ _____

2 $2\frac{1}{4} \times 3\frac{1}{4}$

$\frac{\square}{4} \times \frac{\square}{4} =$ _____

3 $3\frac{1}{3} \times 2\frac{1}{3}$

$\frac{\square}{3} \times \frac{\square}{3} =$ _____

4 $1\frac{1}{2} \times 2\frac{2}{3}$

$\frac{\square}{2} \times \frac{\square}{3} =$ _____

5 $1\frac{1}{3} \times 2\frac{3}{4}$

$\frac{\square}{3} \times \frac{\square}{4} =$ _____

6 $1\frac{1}{4} \times 2\frac{2}{5}$

$\frac{\square}{4} \times \frac{\square}{5} =$ _____

7 $2\frac{1}{2} \times 2\frac{4}{5}$

$\frac{\square}{2} \times \frac{\square}{5} =$ _____

8 $2\frac{1}{4} \times 1\frac{3}{5}$

$\frac{\square}{4} \times \frac{\square}{5} =$ _____

9 $2\frac{1}{8} \times 4\frac{2}{5}$

$\frac{\square}{8} \times \frac{\square}{5} =$ _____

10 $2\frac{3}{4} \times 3\frac{1}{6}$

$\frac{\square}{4} \times \frac{\square}{6} =$ _____

11 $2\frac{2}{3} \times 4\frac{4}{9}$

$\frac{\square}{3} \times \frac{\square}{9} =$ _____

12 $5\frac{1}{5} \times 4\frac{1}{10}$

$\frac{\square}{5} \times \frac{\square}{10} =$ _____

☆ **Tell how you multiply mixed numbers.**

● ● ●

Solve each problem. Write the answer in simplest form. Show your work.

1 The scone recipe calls for $3\frac{3}{4}$ cups of flour. If Charlotte wants to cut the recipe in half, how much flour should she use?

2 Mr. Nichols grows lettuce on his farm. He watered $3\frac{1}{2}$ acres so far today. He also has begun fertilizing $\frac{1}{4}$ of those acres. How many acres of lettuce has he watered and fertilized so far today?

3 Martha made $2\frac{2}{3}$ pounds of pasta. She divided the pasta into fourths. How much pasta is in each portion?

4 Zev is planting a garden. The garden is $10\frac{1}{3}$ yards long and 8 yards wide. What is the area of the garden?

5 Perry's patio is $6\frac{1}{2}$ meters long and $5\frac{2}{3}$ meters wide. What is the area of his patio?

6 Mrs. Rinaldi bought $5\frac{1}{2}$ pounds of apples. She used $\frac{4}{5}$ of that amount to make pies. How many pounds of apples did she use for the pies?

Circle the letter for the correct answer.

7 What is the product of $5\frac{1}{4}$ and $\frac{3}{7}$?

a) 2

b) $2\frac{9}{28}$

c) $2\frac{1}{3}$

d) $2\frac{1}{4}$

8 What is the product of $10\frac{5}{6}$ and $\frac{1}{3}$?

a) $3\frac{11}{18}$

b) $3\frac{1}{9}$

c) $3\frac{5}{18}$

d) $3\frac{5}{9}$

Unit 19
Divide Whole Numbers and Fractions

Standard

Number & Operations—Fractions
Apply and extend previous understandings of multiplication and division to multiply and divide fractions.
5.NF.7 Apply and extend previous understandings of division to divide unit fractions by whole numbers and whole numbers by unit fractions.
    a) Interpret division of a unit fraction by a non-zero whole number, and compute such quotients.
    b) Interpret division of a whole number by a unit fraction, and compute such quotients.
    c) Solve real world problems involving division of unit fractions by non-zero whole numbers and division of whole numbers by unit fractions.

Model the Skill

◆ Write the following problem on the board.

$$3 \div \frac{1}{4} = \underline{\hspace{2cm}}$$

◆ **Say:** *Today we are going to divide a whole number by a fraction. Do you think if I divide a whole number like 3 by a fraction I will have more than 3 pieces or less than 3 pieces?* (more)

◆ **Ask:** *How many circles do you see? How many quarters, or fourths, do you see?* (12) *So 3 divided by 1/4 is equal to 12. Do you agree?* Encourage students to discuss why the quotient is 12, using the art to support their understanding.

◆ Assign students the appropriate practice page(s) to support their understanding of the skill.

Assess the Skill

Use the following problems to pre-/post-assess students' understanding of the skill.

$2 \div \frac{1}{3}$ $3 \div \frac{1}{2}$ $4 \div \frac{1}{5}$ $1 \div \frac{3}{4}$

$6 \div \frac{2}{3}$ $5 \div \frac{7}{10}$ $2 \div \frac{2}{7}$ $9 \div \frac{5}{6}$

Name _____

Find the quotient for each problem.

1 $3 \div \frac{1}{2} =$ _____

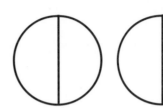

2 $4 \div \frac{1}{3} =$ _____

3 $2 \div \frac{1}{3} =$ _____

4 $5 \div \frac{1}{2} =$ _____

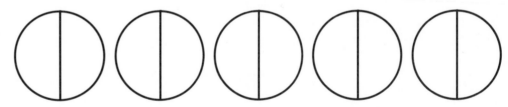

5 $\frac{1}{8} \div 2 =$ _____

6 $\frac{1}{3} \div 3 =$ _____

   Look at Problem 4. Tell how you know the quotient will be more than 5.

Name _____

Find the quotient for each problem.

 1

$\frac{1}{2} \div 3 =$ _____

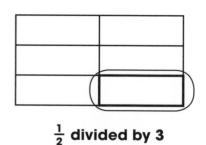

$\frac{1}{2}$ **divided by 3**

2

$4 \div \frac{1}{8} =$ _____

3

$2 \div \frac{1}{5} =$ _____

4

$\frac{1}{3} \div 4 =$ _____

5

$\frac{1}{6} \div 2 =$ _____

6

$\frac{2}{3} \div 2 =$ _____

7

$\frac{3}{7} \div 9 =$ _____

8

$\frac{4}{5} \div 6 =$ _____

9

$\frac{2}{5} \div 4 =$ _____

10

$\frac{3}{5} \div 3 =$ _____

 Look at Problem 9. Tell how you know the quotient will be less than $\frac{1}{5}$.

● ● ○

Divide. If there is a remainder, write it as a fraction.

❶

$2 \div 5 =$ _____

❷

$1 \div 3 =$ _____

$3\overline{)1}$

❸

$3 \div 4 =$ _____

$4\overline{)3}$

❹

$1 \div 5 =$ _____

$5\overline{)1}$

❺

$5 \div 8 =$ _____

$8\overline{)5}$

❻

$3 \div 6 =$ _____

$6\overline{)3}$

❼

$8 \div 6 =$ _____

$6\overline{)8}$

❽

$9 \div 7 =$ _____

$7\overline{)9}$

❾

$13 \div 6 =$ _____

$6\overline{)13}$

❿

$27 \div 5 =$ _____

$5\overline{)27}$

⓫

$17 \div 4 =$ _____

$4\overline{)17}$

⓬

$18 \div 5 =$ _____

$5\overline{)18}$

⓭

$33 \div 6 =$ _____

$6\overline{)33}$

⓮

$28 \div 8 =$ _____

$8\overline{)28}$

⓯

$48 \div 9 =$ _____

$9\overline{)48}$

⓰

$52 \div 5 =$ _____

$5\overline{)52}$

 Look at Problem 16. Explain how you know the remainder will be less than $\frac{5}{5}$.

Solve.

1 The ceramics class had 15 pounds of clay. Each student got $\frac{3}{4}$ of a pound to make a bowl. How many bowls did the students make?

2 Hadley has a $\frac{1}{2}$ kilogram of popcorn. She divides the popcorn into 3 equal bags. How many kilograms of popcorn are in each bag?

3 Rory walks a combined $\frac{7}{8}$ of a mile to school and back each day. How many miles does he walk each way?

4 Jackson has 100 pounds of apples to sell at the farmers' market. If he divides the apples into $2\frac{1}{2}$-pound bags, how many bags will he have to sell?

5 The hike to the campsite is 4 kilometers long. If we each take turns carrying the tent for $\frac{4}{5}$ of a kilometer, how many times will the tent change hands?

6 The pizzeria buys 250 pounds of mozzarella cheese. If they use $20\frac{5}{6}$ pounds of cheese every day, how long will the cheese last?

Circle the letter for the correct answer.

7 What is the quotient of 10 divided by $\frac{3}{5}$?

a) 17

b) 6

c) $16\frac{1}{3}$

d) $16\frac{2}{3}$

8 We had 7 sandwiches. Everyone ate $\frac{1}{4}$ sandwich for a snack. How many people had snacks?

a) $\frac{1}{28}$

b) $6\frac{3}{4}$

c) 28

d) 32

Unit 20
Convert Among Metric Units

Standard

Measurement & Data
Convert like measurement units within a given measurement system.
5.MD.1 Convert among different-sized standard measurement units within a
given measurement system (e.g., convert 5 cm to 0.05 m), and use
these conversions in solving multi-step, real world problems.

Model the Skill

◆ **Ask:** *What are some units of length in the metric system?* Write the units
and their abbreviations on the board (km, m, cm, mm). You may wish to
include decameter (dm). Allow students to examine a cm ruler. Discuss that
a millimeter is 1/10 of a centimeter and relate it to decimal notation. Be sure
students understand the relative size of all the units of length.

◆ **Say:** *When we operate with units of length, we need to work with the same
units, so sometimes we need to convert a smaller unit to a larger unit, or a
larger unit to a smaller unit.*

◆ **Ask:** *How can we convert meters into centimeters?* (multiply by 100) *How can
we convert centimeters into meters?* (divide by 100) Help students understand
that when we multiply to convert from a larger unit to a smaller unit, we will get
more smaller units. Conversely, when we divide, we will get fewer (or a part of)
large units.

◆ Assign students the appropriate practice page(s) to support their
understanding of the skill.

Assess the Skill

**Use the following problems to pre-/post-assess students' understanding of
the skill.**

◆ Ask students to convert the following measurements to complete the table.

Metric Units of Length				
10 millimeters			0.01 meter	0.00001 kilometer
100 millimeters	10 centimeters			0.0001 kilometer
1,000 millimeters			1 meter	
				1 kilometer

Name _____

Complete each problem. Use the chart to help you.

Metric Units of Length

1   3,000 centimeters (cm) = _____ meters (m)

Divide: 3,000 ÷ 100 = _____

x 1,000

1 km = 1,000 m

1 m = 0.001 km

÷ 1,000

2   50 millimeters (mm) = _____ centimeters (cm)

Divide: _____ ÷ _____ = _____

3   8 kilometers (km) = _____ meters (m)

Multiply: 8 x 1,000 = _____

x 100

1 m = 100 cm

1 cm = 0.01 m

÷ 100

4   85 meters (m) = _____ kilometers (km)

5   17 centimeters (cm) = _____ meter (m)

Divide: 17 ÷ 100 = _____

x 10

1 cm = 10 mm

1 mm = 0.1 cm

÷ 10

6   6 millimeters (mm) = _____ centimeters (cm)

Divide: _____ ÷ _____ = _____

☆   **Tell how you can convert meters to kilometers.**

Complete each problem. Use the chart to help you.

Metric Units of Mass

1 20 kilograms (kg) = _____ metric tons (t)

_____ ÷ _____ = _____

2 1,300 grams (g) = _____ kilograms (kg)

1 t = 1,000 kg
1 kg = 0.001 t

3 9 kg = _____ g

_____ x _____ = _____

4 50 kg = _____ t

1 kg = 1,000 g
1 g = 0.001 kg

5 4,020 kg = _____ t

6 7 g = _____ kg

7 30 kg = _____ g

8 10,500 kg = _____ t

☆ **Tell how you know your answer is correct.**

Name _____

Complete each problem. Use the chart to help you.

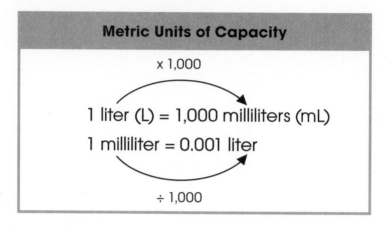

Metric Units of Capacity

x 1,000

1 liter (L) = 1,000 milliliters (mL)
1 milliliter = 0.001 liter

÷ 1,000

1 5 mL = _____ L

2 360 mL = _____ L

3 2,850 mL = _____ L

4 1,900 mL = _____ L

5 70 mL = _____ L

6 305 mL = _____ L

7 6 L = _____ mL

8 807 L = _____ mL

9 25.5 L = _____ mL

10 1,100 mL = _____ L

11 450 mL = _____ L

12 10 mL = _____ L

 Tell what to do when you want to convert from a smaller unit to a larger unit.

Solve each problem. Show your work.

1 The fish aquarium holds 150 liters of water. How many milliliters does the aquarium hold?

2 The mass of the boulder is 48,567 kilograms. What is the mass of the boulder in metric tons?

3 The pier is 200 meters long. Each board is 80 centimeters wide. How many boards are in the pier?

4 We rode our bikes 3,500 meters every day for 5 days. How many kilometers did we bike in all?

5 Felice caught 5.4 kilograms of fish this morning. Her dad caught 3,900 grams. How many kilograms of fish did they catch in all?

6 It is a 3-kilometer hike to the river. PJ walks for 500 meters. Then he walks another 1,050 meters. How many more kilometers must PJ hike to reach the river?

Circle the letter for the correct answer.

7 How many milliliters are in 35.05 liters?

a) 0.3505

b) 30,505

c) 35,500

d) 35,050

8 How many millimeters are in 20 meters?

a) 0.02

b) 2,000

c) 20,000

d) 200,000

Unit 21
Convert Among Customary Units

Standard

Measurement & Data
Convert like measurement units within a given measurement system.
5.MD.1 Convert among different-sized standard measurement units within a given measurement system (e.g., convert 5 cm to 0.05 m), and use these conversions in solving multi-step, real world problems.

Model the Skill

Customary Units of Length	
12 inches (in) = 1 foot (ft)	36 inches = 1 yard
3 feet = 1 yard (yd)	5,280 feet = 1 mile (mi)

◆ **Ask:** *What are some units of length in the customary system?* Write the units and their abbreviations on the board (in, ft, yd, mi). Be sure students understand the relative size of all the units of length.

◆ **Say:** *When we operate with units of length in the customary system, we often mix units, like 5 feet 6 inches, or we use fractions, like $5\frac{1}{2}$ feet.* Have students look at the chart and discuss equivalents. Note that they are not powers of ten like in the metric system.

◆ **Ask:** *When we need to convert a smaller unit to a larger unit, what do you think we do?* (divide) *How many feet is 60 inches?* (5 ft) *What did you use as the divisor?* (12) *When we need to convert a larger unit to a smaller unit, what do you think we do?* (multiply) *How many feet is 4 yards?* (12 ft) *What did you use as the multiplier?* (3)

◆ Assign students the appropriate practice page(s) to support their understanding of the skill.

Assess the Skill

Use the following problems to pre-/post-assess students' understanding of the skill.

◆ Ask students to convert the following measurements to complete the table.

Customary Units of Length		
12 inches	1 foot	$\frac{1}{3}$ yard
36 inches		1 yard
5,280 feet		1 mile

Complete each problem.

Customary Units of Length	
12 inches (in) = 1 foot (ft)	36 inches = 1 yard
3 feet = 1 yard (yd)	5,280 feet = 1 mile (mi)

1 48 inches = _____ feet

Divide: 48 ÷ 12 = _____

2 132 inches = _____ feet

Divide: 132 ÷ 12 = _____

3 54 feet = _____ yards

_____ ÷ _____ = _____

4 96 feet = _____ yards

_____ ÷ _____ = _____

5 4 yd = _____ in

Multiply: 4 x _____ = _____

6 50 yd = _____ ft

Multiply: 3 x _____ = _____

7 10 ft = _____ yd

10 ft = _____ yd _____ ft

8 272 ft = _____ yd

272 ft = _____ yd _____ ft

 Tell how you can convert feet to yards.

Name _____

Complete each problem.

Customary Units of Weight
16 ounces (oz) = 1 pound (lb)
2,000 pounds = 1 ton (t)

1 6,000 lb = _____ t

_____ ÷ _____ = _____

2 10,000 lb = _____ t

---

3 64 oz = _____ lb

4 100 oz = _____ lb

_____ lb and _____ oz

---

5 15 t = _____ lb

_____ x _____ = _____

6 2 t = ___ oz

_____ x _____ x _____ = _____

---

7 $1\frac{1}{2}$ t = _____ lb

8 $3\frac{1}{4}$ t = _____ lb

---

9 28 oz = _____ lb

10 5,000 lb = _____ t

---

11 32 t = _____ lb

12 65 oz = _____ lb

 Tell how you know your answer is correct.

●●○

Complete each problem.

Customary Units of Capacity	
8 fluid ounces (fl oz) = 1 cup (c)	2 pints = 1 quart (qt)
2 cups = 1 pint (pt)	4 quarts = 1 gallon (gal)

1 48 fl oz = _____ c

2 4 fl oz = _____ c

3 98 fl oz = _____ c

4 32 c = _____ pt

5 16 c = _____ qt

6 20 qt = _____ gal

7 2 gal = _____ qt

8 50 pt = _____ c

9 54 qt = _____ pt

10 1 gal = _____ oz

11 424 pt = _____ gal

12 10 gal = _____ qt

 Tell what to do when you want to convert from a smaller unit to a larger unit.

Solve each problem. Draw a picture to help you. Show your work.

1 The window is 60 inches wide. What is the width of the window in feet?

2 The perimeter of Jared's property is 56 yards. How many feet of fence will Jared need if he wants to enclose the whole property?

3 Each serving of oatmeal is 8 ounces. How many servings are in a 5-lb bag of oats?

4 The bottle of water contains 32 fluid ounces of water. How many cups of water are in the bottle?

5 We have 8 yards of wrapping paper. If we use 2 feet for each present, how many presents can we wrap?

6 Stephanie rides her bike 2 miles to the post office, and then another 50 yards to the train station. How many yards long was her trip?

Circle the letter for the correct answer.

7 How many gallons are in 500 pints?

a) 125
b) 62.5
c) 1,000
d) 4,000

8 If there are 5,280 feet in one mile, how many yards are in 2 miles?

a) 1,760
b) 10,560
c) 35,200
d) 3,520

Unit 22
Use Measurement Data

Standard

Measurement & Data
Convert like measurement units within a given measurement system.
5.MD.2 Make a line plot to display a data set of measurements in fractions of a unit (1/2, 1/4, 1/8). Use operations on fractions for this grade to solve problems involving information presented in line plots.

Model the Skill

◆ Draw the following line plot on the board.

Length of Sea Tortoises (in feet)

```
                    X
              X     X           X
        X     X     X     X     X
  X     X     X     X     X     X
+-----+-----+-----+-----+-----+-----+
  2     3     4     5     6     7     8
```

◆ **Ask:** *What do you know about graphs? Why do we use graphs?* Record students' responses on the board.

◆ **Say:** *Today we are going to look at a graph called a line plot.* Have students look at the line plot and discuss. Help students understand that the scale is a number line and that each X records the value of one data point. The stack of Xs shows the frequency.

◆ **Ask:** *What are the lengths of the tortoises? Where do you see that information?* (3–8 feet; on the scale at the bottom of the graph)

◆ Point out that the number (or numbers) that occurs most often in a data set is called the mode. Students should count the number of Xs to determine how many tortoises are in the data set.

◆ Assign students the appropriate practice page(s) to support their understanding of the skill.

Assess the Skill

Use the following activity to pre-/post-assess students' understanding of the skill.

◆ Ask students to conduct a class survey to collect data. Data sets could include height, size, number of siblings, number of pets, etc. Have students use their data to make a line plot to present.

Name _____

Use the graph to answer the questions.

Weight of Chestnuts (in ounces)

```
                          x
              x           x
              x           x           x
   x          x           x           x
   x          x           x           x           x
   x          x           x           x           x           x
 --+----------+-----------+-----------+-----------+-----------+---
   1                      2                       3                       4
```

1 What information does the graph show?

_____

2 Why do you think this type of graph is called a line plot?

_____

_____

3 How many chestnuts weigh $1\frac{1}{2}$ ounces? _____

_____

4 What is the weight that occurred most often? _____

_____

5 What is the weight that occurred least often?

_____

6 How many chestnuts were weighed? _____

☆ **Circle the answer that shows the mode.**

Use the graph to answer the questions.

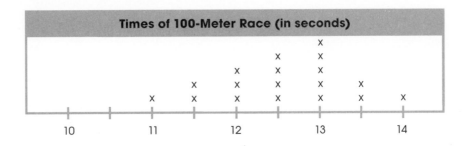

Times of 100-Meter Race (in seconds)

❶ What does the line plot show?

_____

_____

❷ What was the mode of the race?

_____

_____

❸ How many athletes ran in the race?

_____

❹ What is the fastest value?

_____

❺ What is the slowest value?

_____

❻ What is the difference between the fastest value and the slowest value?

_____

❼ What is the median in this set of data?

_____

❽ What is the mean in this set of data?

_____

☆ **Tell how you found the median.**

Name _____

Use the graph to answer the questions.

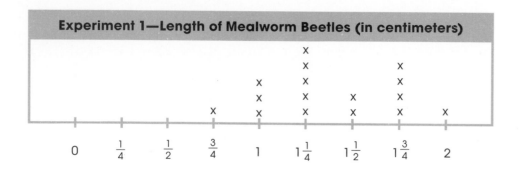

1 What does the line plot show?

_____

_____

2 What is the mode of the data set?

_____

_____

3 How many mealworms were measured for the experiment?

_____

4 What is the median of the data set?

_____

_____

5 What is the greatest value in the data set?

_____

6 What is the least value in the data set?

_____

7 What is the range of the data?

_____

8 What is the mean of the data set?

_____

☆ **Tell how you solved the problem.**

●●●

Name _____

Complete the line plot below with the data in the table. Then answer the questions.

cm	Frequency
$\frac{1}{2}$	I
$\frac{3}{4}$	IIII
1	I
$1\frac{1}{4}$	III
$1\frac{1}{2}$	II
2	I

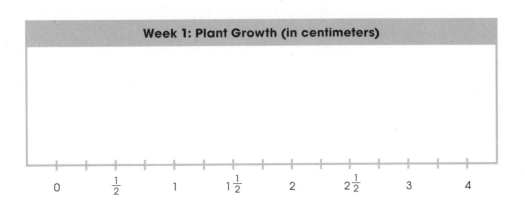

2 What does the line plot show?

_____

_____

3 What was the mode of the data set?

_____

_____

4 How many plants were measured?

_____

5 What is the greatest value in the data set?

_____

6 What is the least value in the data set?

a) 1

b) $\frac{1}{2}$

c) $\frac{1}{4}$

d) 0

7 What is the difference between the least value and greatest value?

a) $\frac{1}{2}$

b) $1\frac{1}{2}$

c) 2

d) 3

Unit 23
Understand Volume

Standard

Measurement & Data
Geometric measurement: understand concepts of volume and relate volume to multiplication and to addition.
5.MD.3 Recognize volume as an attribute of solid figures and understand concepts of volume measurement.
   a) A cube with side length 1 unit, called a "unit cube," is said to have "one cubic unit" of volume, and can be used to measure volume.
   b) A solid figure which can be packed without gaps or overlaps using *n* unit cubes is said to have a volume of *n* cubic units.
5.MD.4 Measure volumes by counting unit cubes, using cubic cm, cubic in, cubic ft, and improvised units.

Model the Skill

◆ **Say:** *Today we are going measure volume. All solid shapes have volume. Who can tell me what volume is?* Record and discuss students' responses. Help students understand that a solid figure can be "packed" with cubic units, and that volume is the number of the cubic units that fill the figure without gaps or overlaps.

◆ **Say:** *How do you describe a cubic unit?* (Possible response: Each edge measures 1 unit, like 1 cm.) Have students use cm cubes to build different shapes and count the number of cubic units to find the volume.

◆ Assign students the appropriate practice page(s) to support their understanding of the skill.

Assess the Skill

Use the following problems to pre-/post-assess students' understanding of the skill.

◆ Ask students to find the volume of the following boxes.

   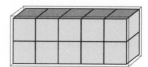

Count the cubic units to find the volume.

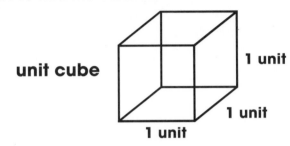

unit cube

1 unit

1 unit

1 unit

1 The volume is _____ cubic units.

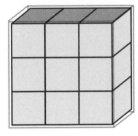

2 The volume is _____ cubic units.

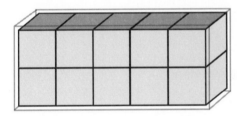

3 The volume is _____ cubic units.

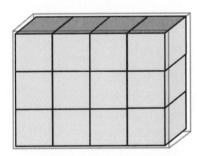

4 The volume is _____ cubic units.

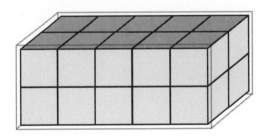

☆ **Draw a circle around the figure with the greatest volume.**

Name _____

Find the volume of each box.

1 cubic centimeter

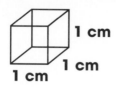

1 cm
1 cm
1 cm

1 The volume is _____ cubic cm.

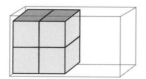

2 The volume is _____ cubic cm.

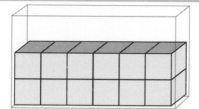

3 The volume is _____ cubic cm.

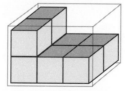

4 The volume is _____ cubic cm.

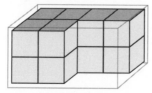

5 The volume is _____ cubic cm.

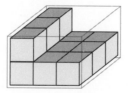

6 The volume is _____ cubic cm.

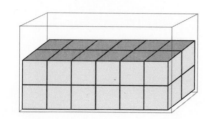

 Tell how you found the volume.

Find the volume.

❶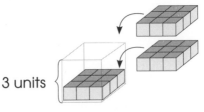

3 units

Number of cubic units in one layer: ____

Number of layers: ____

Volume: ____ + ____ + ____ = _____

❷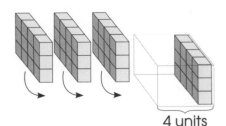

4 units

Number of cubic units in one layer: ____

Number of layers: ____

Volume: ____ + ____ + ____ + ____ = _____

❸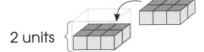

2 units

Number of cubic units in one layer: ____

Number of layers: ____

Volume: ____ x ____ = _____

❹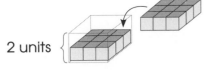

2 units

Number of cubic units in one layer: ____

Number of layers: ____

Volume: ____ x ____ = _____

❺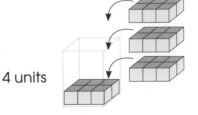

4 units

Number of cubic units in one layer: ____

Number of layers: ____

Volume: _____

❻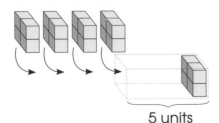

5 units

Number of cubic units in one layer: ____

Number of layers: ____

Volume: _____

❼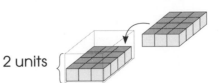

2 units

Number of cubic units in one layer: ____

Number of layers: ____

Volume: _____

❽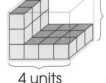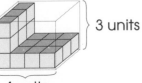

3 units

4 units

Number of cubic units in one layer: ____

Number of layers: ____

Volume: _____

 Tell how you solved the problem.

Solve each problem. Show your work.

1 Six cubic units fit in one layer of a box. The box holds four layers. What is the volume of the box?

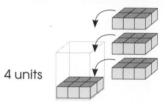

4 units

2 If 12 cubic units fill the bottom layer of a box, and the box holds 3 layers, what is the volume of the box?

3 If 3 cubic centimeters fill the bottom layer of a box, and the box fits 6 layers, what is the volume of the box?

4 The gift box fits 2 layers of 10 cubic inches. What is the volume of the box?

5 What is the volume of the box?

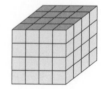

6 What is the volume of this box?

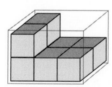

Circle the letter for the correct answer.

7 Which rectangular prism has the least volume?

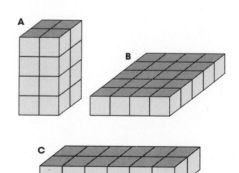

8 The volume of a cube-shaped box is 81 cubic centimeters. If the bottom layer of the box fits 9 cubic centimeters, how many more layers can fit in the box?

a) 72

b) 81

c) 8

d) 9

Unit 24
Find Volume

Standard

Measurement & Data
Geometric measurement: understand concepts of volume and relate volume to multiplication and to addition.
5.MD.4 Measure volumes by counting unit cubes, using cubic cm, cubic in, cubic ft, and improvised units.
5.MD.5 Relate volume to the operations of multiplication and addition and solve real world and mathematical problems involving volume.

Model the Skill

◆ Draw the following problem on the board.

◆ **Say:** *Today we are going to find the volume of rectangular prisms by using a formula.* Have students look at the problem and identify the rectangular prism, the height, and the base.

height: 3 cm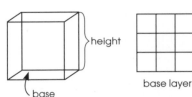

◆ **Ask:** *If we use centimeter cubes, how many cubes form the bottom layer of this prism?* (9) Tell students that the bottom layer is called the base. **Ask:** *If I want to find the area of the base, what should I do?* (multiply length times width) Remind students that area tells the number of square units, and that it is not until they multiply by height (the third dimension) that they find cubic units of volume.

◆ Allow students to use cm cubes to model the problems, proving that the area of the base times the height yields the same answer as counting cubes and layers. Then assign students the appropriate practice page(s) to support their understanding of the skill.

Assess the Skill

Use the following problems to pre-/post-assess students' understanding of the skill.

◆ Ask students to use formulas to find the volume of the following solids.

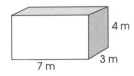

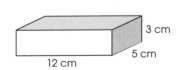

Name _____

Find the volume of each rectangular prism.

1 Area of the base: _____ sq cm

Height: 4 cm

Volume: _____ x _____ = _____

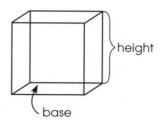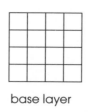

2 Area of the base: _____ sq m

Height: _____

Volume: _____ x _____ = _____

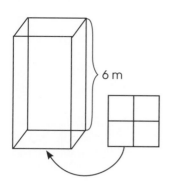

3 Area of the base: _____ sq ft

Height: _____

Volume: _____ x _____ = _____

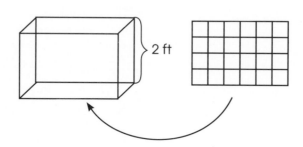

4 Area of the base: _____ sq ft

Height: _____

Volume: _____ x _____ = _____

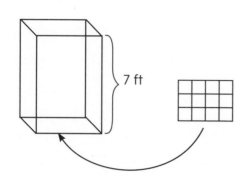

  Tell how you can use area to find volume.

Use a formula to find volume. Show your work.

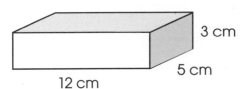

Formulas for Volume of a Rectangular Prism	
Volume = base (area of) x height	$V = b \times h$
Volume = length x width x height	$V = l \times w \times h$

Remember:
You can multiply in any order.

❶ length _____ width _____ height _____

area of base _____

Volume _____

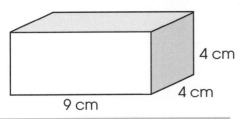
3 cm
5 cm
12 cm

❷ length _____ width _____ height _____

area of base _____

Volume _____

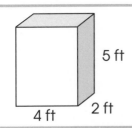
5 ft
4 ft   2 ft

❸ length _____ width _____ height _____

area of base _____

Volume _____

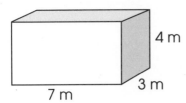
4 m
7 m   3 m

❹ length _____ width _____ height _____

area of base _____

Volume _____

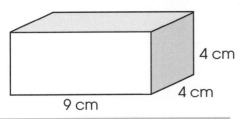
4 cm
9 cm   4 cm

❺ length _____ width _____ height _____

area of base _____

Volume _____

10 m
10 m
10 m

❻ length _____ width _____ height _____

area of base _____

Volume _____

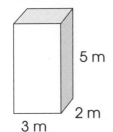
5 m
3 m   2 m

 Tell how you found the volume.

Name _____

Find the missing dimension. Use the formula V = l x w x h.

1 V = ____ x ____ x ____

V = ____ x ____

V = ____

V = ____

V = ?

4 cm

4 cm

5 cm

2 V = ____ x ____ x ____

V = ____ x ____

V = ____

V = ____

V = ?

4 ft

10 ft   5 ft

3 96 = ____ x ____ x h

96 = ____ x h

h = 96 ÷ ____

h = ____

V = 96 cu m

h = ?

8 m   4 m

4 56 = ____ x ____ x h

56 = ____ x h

h = 56 ÷ ____

h = ____

V = 56 cu cm

h = ?

7 cm   4 cm

5 125 = ____ x w x ____

125 = ____ x w

w = 125 ÷ ____

w = ____

V = 125 cu cm

5 cm

5 cm   w = ?

6 180 = ____ x w x ____

180 = ____ x w

w = 180 ÷ ____

w = ____

V = 180 cu in

5 in

12 in   w = ?

7 72 = l x ____ x ____

72 = l x ____

l = ____ ÷ ____

l = ____

V = 72 cu cm

8 cm

3 cm

l = ?

8 320 = l x ____ x ____

320 = l x ____

l = ____ ÷ ____

l = ____

V = 320 cu cm

10 cm

4 cm

l = ?

9 360 = ____ x w x ____

360 = ____ x w

w = 360 ÷ ____

w = ____

V = 360 cu units

9 units

10 units   n units

10 80 = 10 x ____ x h

80 = ____ x h

h = 80 ÷ ____

h = ____

V = 80

h = ?

4 cm

4 cm

☆ **Tell how you solved the problem.**

Name _____

Solve each problem. Show your work.

1 Matt wants to mail a book that is 8 inches long, 5 inches wide, and 2 inches thick. What is the smallest possible volume of a box that the book will fit in?

2 The area of the base a box is 9 square units. If the height of the box is 10 units, what is the volume of the box?

3 The refrigerator box is 6 feet tall, 4 feet deep, and 4 feet wide. What is the volume of the box?

4 The gift box is 10 centimeters by 12 centimeters by 3 centimeters. What is the volume of the box?

5 The dimensions of a large pizza box are 16 in x 16 in x 2 in. What is the volume of the box?

6 The base area of the suitcase is 308 square inches. If the height of the suitcase is 9 inches, what is the volume of the suitcase?

Circle the letter for the correct answer.

7 What is the volume of this rectangular prism?

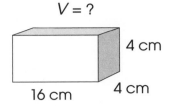

$V = ?$

16 cm   4 cm   4 cm

a) 64 sq cm
b) 128 sq cm
c) 256 sq cm
d) 256 cu cm

8 The volume of a cube-shaped box is 27 cubic centimeters. What is the height of the box?

a) 7 cm
b) 8 cm
c) 9 cm
d) 3 cm

Unit 25
Locate Points on the Coordinate Plane

Standard

Geometry
Graph points on the coordinate plane to solve real world and mathematical problems.

5.G.1 Use a pair of perpendicular number lines, called axes, to define a coordinate system, with the intersection of the lines (the origin) arranged to coincide with the 0 on each line and a given point in the plane located by using an ordered pair of numbers, called its coordinates. Understand that the first number indicates how far to travel from the origin in the direction of one axis, and the second number indicates how far to travel in the direction of the second axis, with the convention that the names of the two axes and the coordinates correspond.

5.G.2 Represent real world and mathematical problems by graphing points in the first quadrant of the coordinate plane, and interpret coordinate values of points in the context of the situation.

Model the Skill

◆ Draw the coordinate plane on the board and plot the following points.

◆ **Ask:** *What do you know about a coordinate plane? What are coordinates? How are they used?* Record students' responses. Tell students that the plane is two-dimensional space and coordinates are the numbers that let us locate points in that space, like coordinates on a map or GPS.

◆ Have students look at the board and point to the grid, the lines or axes that form the grid, the horizontal *x*-axis, the vertical *y*-axis, and the origin where the axes meet.

◆ **Say:** *We use ordered pairs to locate points. Ordered pairs are coordinates. The first number (x) tells how far to move along the x-axis. The second number in the ordered pair (y) tells how far to move along the y-axis.* Point A is at (2, 4). Have students locate the points at (4, 2) and (3, 1). Emphasize that order is important.

◆ Assign students the appropriate practice page(s) to support their understanding of the skill.

Assess the Skill

Use the following problems to pre-/post-assess students' understanding of the skill.

◆ Have students write ordered pairs for additional points on the coordinate plane.

Write what is located at each point.

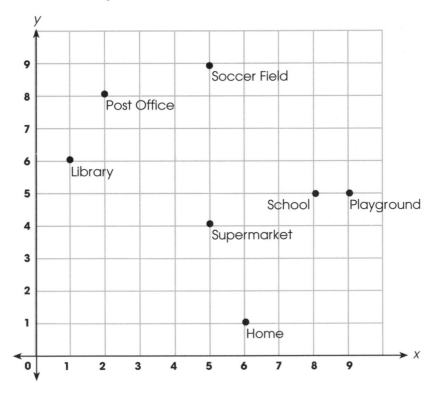

①

x	y
6	1

_____

②

x	y
9	5

_____

③

x	y
5	9

_____

④

x	y
8	5

_____

⑤

x	y
1	6

_____

⑥

x	y
2	8

_____

 Circle the ordered pair that has the opposite set of coordinates from the library.

Name _____

Write the ordered pair for each point.

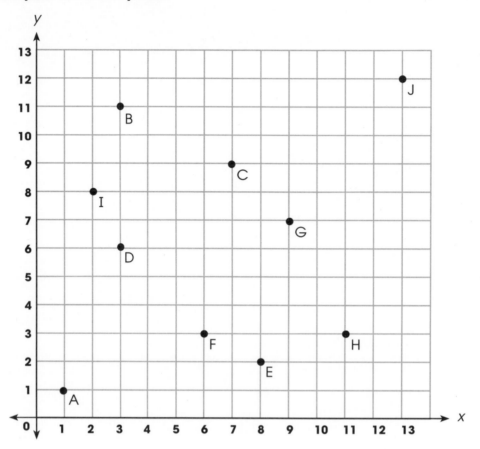

1 Point A: (1, _____)

2 Point B: (3, _____)

3 Point C: (_____, _____)

4 Point D: (_____, _____)

5 Point E: (_____, _____)

6 Point F: (_____, _____)

7 Point G: (_____, _____)

8 Point H: (_____, _____)

9 Point I: (_____, _____)

10 Point J: (_____, _____)

☆ **Tell how you write an ordered pair.**

●●○

Write the ordered pair for each point.

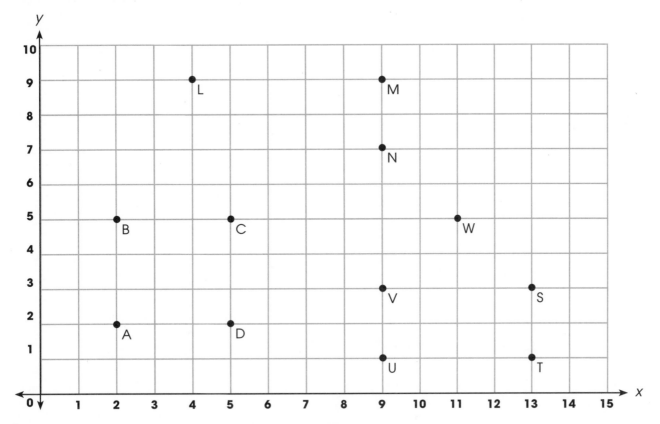

1️⃣ Point A: (_____ , _____)

2️⃣ Point B: (_____ , _____)

3️⃣ Point C: (_____ , _____)

4️⃣ Point D: (_____ , _____)

5️⃣ Point L: (_____ , _____)

6️⃣ Point M: (_____ , _____)

7️⃣ Point N: (_____ , _____)

8️⃣ Point S: (_____ , _____)

9️⃣ Point T: (_____ , _____)

🔟 Point U: (_____ , _____)

1️⃣1️⃣ Point V: (_____ , _____)

1️⃣2️⃣ Point W: (_____ , _____)

1️⃣3️⃣ Connect points ABCD and describe

the shape: _____

1️⃣4️⃣ Connect points LMN and describe

the shape: _____

1️⃣5️⃣ Connect points STUVW and describe

the shape: _____

  Explain why the number of points can help you predict the type of polygon.

Use the graph to solve the problems.

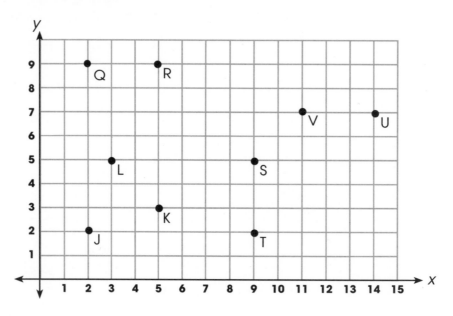

1 Write the ordered pair for point K.

2 Write the ordered pair for point L.

3 What ordered pair describes the location of point R?

4 What point has coordinates (14, 7)?

5 Connect points JKL and describe the shape.

6 What points can you connect to form a trapezoid?

Circle the letter for the correct answer.

7 Which point is located at (5, 9)?

a) Point K

b) Point L

c) Point S

d) Point R

8 What ordered pair describes the location of point V?

a) (14, 7)

b) (11, 7)

c) (12, 7)

d) (7, 11)

Unit 26
Graph Points on the Coordinate Plane

Geometry
Graph points on the coordinate plane to solve real world and mathematical problems.

5.G.1 Use a pair of perpendicular number lines, called axes, to define a coordinate system, with the intersection of the lines (the origin) arranged to coincide with the 0 on each line and a given point in the plane located by using an ordered pair of numbers, called its coordinates. Understand that the first number indicates how far to travel from the origin in the direction of one axis, and the second number indicates how far to travel in the direction of the second axis, with the convention that the names of the two axes and the coordinates correspond.

5.G.2 Represent real world and mathematical problems by graphing points in the first quadrant of the coordinate plane, and interpret coordinate values of points in the context of the situation.

Model the Skill

◆ Draw the coordinate plane on the board and list the following coordinates in written and table form.

x	y
3	5
5	6
7	7
9	8

A (3, 5)   B (5, 6)   C (7, 7)   D (9, 8)

◆ **Say:** *We can use ordered pairs, or coordinates, to plot points. The first number (x) tells how far to move along the x-axis. The second number in the ordered pair (y) tells how far to move along the y-axis. Point A is at (3, 5).* Have students plot points A–D and connect the points to form a line.

◆ Assign students the appropriate practice page(s) to support their understanding of the skill.

Assess the Skill

Use the following problems to pre-/post-assess students' understanding of the skill.

◆ Have students graph the following coordinates on the coordinate plane.

A (3, 5)
B (5, 3)
C (8, 5)
D (6, 7)

x	y
1	2
2	4
3	6
4	8

x	y
3	2
5	4
7	6
9	8

Name _____

Graph and label the following points using the (x, y) coordinates.

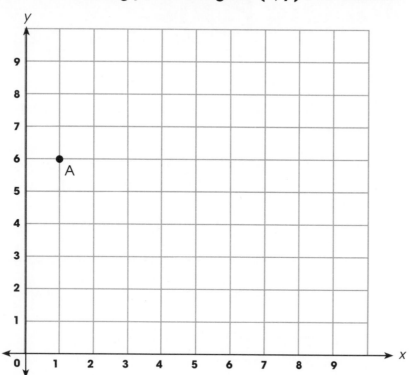

Remember, x is the first number; y is the second number.

① Point A

x	y
1	6

② Point B

x	y
4	6

③ Point C

x	y
4	3

④ Point D

x	y
1	3

⑤ Point E

x	y
2	8

⑥ Point F

x	y
8	2

 Connect points ABCD. What type of shape is ABCD?

Graph and label the following points using the (x, y) coordinates.

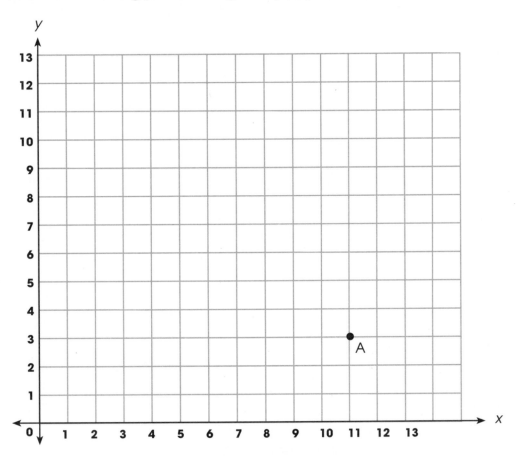

1 Point A: (11, 3)

2 Point B: (11, 5)

3 Point C: (8, 5)

4 Point D: (8, 3)

5 Point E: (2, 12)

6 Point F: (12, 2)

7

hours (x)	3	4	5	6
dollars (y)	5	6	7	8

8

x	y
6	12
8	10
10	8
12	6

☆ **Tell how you use an ordered pair to graph a point.**

Name _____

Graph each point.

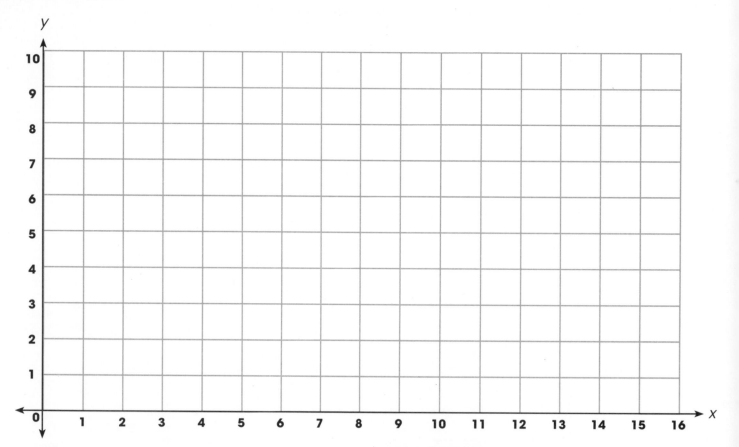

1 Point J: (1, 7)

2 Point K: (2, 9)

3 Point L: (4, 9)

4 Point M: (5, 7)

5 Point N: (4, 5)

6 Point O: (2, 5)

7 Connect points JKLM and describe the shape.

8

quarts (x)	4	8	12	16
gallons (y)	1	2	3	4

9

pints (x)	2	4	6	8
quarts (y)	1	2	3	4

10

x	y
11	9
11	8
11	7
11	6

☆ **Explain why K is a point, KL is a line segment, and y = 9 is a line.**

Solve.

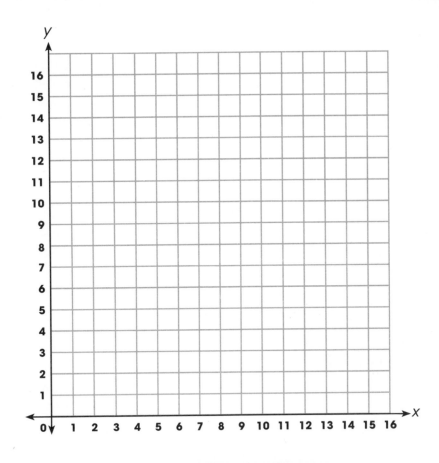

① Use the ordered pair in the table to graph point A on the coordinate plane.

x	y
1	7

② Graph triangle DEF using the following coordinates: (4, 2), (8, 2) and (8, 4)

③ Graph the line $x = y + 1$ using the coordinates in the table.

x	2	3	4	5
y	1	2	3	4

④ In 1 hour, factory workers can make 4 cars. In 2 hours, they can make 8 cars. In 4 hours, they can make 16 cars. Complete the table. Then graph the points in the table.

input	output
x	y
1	4
2	
3	
4	

Circle the letter for the correct answer.

⑤ How many cars can the factory workers make in 10 hours?

a) 10

b) 40

c) 48

d) 56

⑥ Which of the following points is on the line $y = 4x$?

a) (8, 2)

b) (4, 12)

c) (5, 20)

d) (20,5)

Unit 27
Classify Polygons

Geometry
Classify two-dimensional figures into categories based on their properties.

5.G.3. Understand that attributes belonging to a category of two-dimensional figures also belong to all subcategories of that category. For example, all rectangles have four right angles and squares are rectangles, so all squares have four right angles.

5.G.4. Classify two-dimensional figures in a hierarchy based on properties.

Model the Skill

◆ **Say:** *We are going to use properties of polygons.* Remind students that a polygon is a closed, flat shape with sides that are line segments. Have students list the names of as many polygons as they can.

◆ **Ask:** *What are some properties of polygons?* (number of sides and angles, congruent sides, parallel sides, right angles)

◆ Assign students the appropriate practice page(s) to support their understanding of the skill.

Assess the Skill

Use the following problems to pre-/post-assess students' understanding of the skill.

◆ Ask students to describe the following lines and angles.

◆ Ask students to label, sort, and classify the following figures and shapes.

◆ Ask students to define and draw examples of the following:

parallel	quadrilateral
perpendicular	trapezoid
right angle	rhombus
rectangle	similar
	congruent
	line of symmetry

Name _____

Match. Draw a line from one figure to each description.

1 angle

2 congruent

3 parallel

4 parallelogram

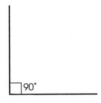

5 quadrilateral

6 rectangle

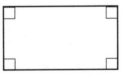

7 right angle

8 perpendicular

☆ **Tell what *parallel* means.**

Name _____

Use the dot paper to draw the figures.

1 Draw two different polygons that have four sides and four angles.

2 Draw two different quadrilaterals that have two pairs of congruent and parallel sides.

3 Draw a quadrilateral with exactly one pair of parallel sides.

4 Draw two similar triangles.

 Tell how a rectangle is different from the quadrilateral you drew.

Draw each figure.

1 a parallelogram with four right angles

2 a parallelogram with no right angles

3 a parallelogram with four congruent sides and four right angles

4 a parallelogram with two congruent sides and two congruent angles

5 a parallelogram with four congruent sides and two pairs of congruent angles

6 a quadrilateral with two parallel sides and two pairs of congruent angles

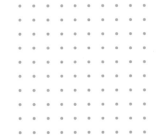

 Describe the properties of a parallelogram.

Name _____

Classify each polygon into categories. Write as many categories that apply.

1 What are three names for a polygon that has four equal sides and no right angles?

_____

_____

2 What is the name of a polygon that has four sides and four equal angles?

_____

_____

3 Draw a polygon with only two congruent sides and two congruent angles.

4 Draw a polygon with only one set of parallel sides and no right angles.

Circle the letter for the correct answer.

5 Which of the following is not a defining property of parallelograms?

  a) four sides and four angles

  b) at least 1 set of parallel sides

  c) at least 1 set of equal angles

  d) at least 1 set of right angles

6 How would you describe the two figures below?

  a) similar

  b) congruent

  c) parallel

  d) perpendicular

Solve.

1 286
   x 2

2 204
   x 8

3 463
   x 78

4 205
   x 635

5 5 x 236

6 7 x 33

7 523 x 3

8 8 x 203

9 452 x 28

10 36 x 328

11 49 x 789

12 10 x 788

13 29 x 211

14 34 x 305

15 8 x 816

16 601 x 19

17 241 x 59

18 809 x 32

19 72 x 407

20 503 x 28

21 602 x 24

22 36 x 126

23 87 x 183

24 64 x 206

25 431 x 33

26 455 x 15

27 67 x 735

28 501 x 12

29 492 x 35

30 39 x 781

31 472 x 237

32 614 x 208

Name _____

Solve.

1 573 x 7   **2** 235 x 6   **3** 514 x 3   **4** 634 x 8

5 423 x 4   **6** 971 x 5   **7** 173 x 9   **8** 308 x 6

9 610 x 10   **10** 34 x 190   **11** 16 x 52   **12** 61 x 189

13 289 x 40   **14** 600 x 33   **15** 388 x 17   **16** 900 x 11

17 672 x 34   **18** 592 x 3   **19** 446 x 63   **20** 806 x 35

21 74 x 109   **22** 38 x 210   **23** 632 x 50   **24** 802 x 100

25 22 x 401   **26** 56 x 439   **27** 72 x 674   **28** 25 x 450

29 60 x 731   **30** 16 x 309   **31** 711 x 711   **32** 53 x 826

Solve.

1 3 x 708

2 15 x 609

3 4 x 413

4 64 x 80

5 473 x 50

6 61 x 517

7 13 x 902

8 83 x 156

9 302 x 60

10 394 x 30

11 165 x 21

12 861 x 29

13 23 x 405

14 611 x 20

15 39 x 178

16 55 x 230

17 62 x 934

18 92 x 209

19 115 x 79

20 205 x 45

21 73 x 515

22 308 x 12

23 60 x 252

24 266 x 30

25 201 x 413

26 560 x 39

27 732 x 24

28 425 x 104

29 609 x 315

30 168 x 759

31 382 x 296

32 513 x 169

Name _____

Solve.

1   574 ÷ 7   **2**   240 ÷ 6   **3**   513 ÷ 3   **4**   636 ÷ 8

5   426 ÷ 4   **6**   970 ÷ 5   **7**   189 ÷ 9   **8**   303 ÷ 6

9   610 ÷ 10   **10**   340 ÷ 170   **11**   312 ÷ 52   **12**   756 ÷ 189

13   300 ÷ 40   **14**   600 ÷ 8   **15**   357 ÷ 17   **16**   990 ÷ 11

17   646 ÷ 34   **18**   592 ÷ 40   **19**   448 ÷ 16   **20**   805 ÷ 35

21   228 ÷ 19   **22**   840 ÷ 21   **23**   640 ÷ 50   **24**   802 ÷ 10

25   2,205 ÷ 401   **26**   462 ÷ 44   **27**   704 ÷ 64   **28**   2,250 ÷ 55

29   780 ÷ 65   **30**   409 ÷ 50   **31**   770 ÷ 80   **32**   533 ÷ 41

Name _____

Solve.

1 708 ÷ 3   **2** 609 ÷ 15   **3** 413 ÷ 4   **4** 800 ÷ 64

5 475 ÷ 50   **6** 663 ÷ 13   **7** 910 ÷ 70   **8** 936 ÷ 156

9 840 ÷ 14   **10** 375 ÷ 30   **11** 252 ÷ 21   **12** 870 ÷ 29

13 504 ÷ 45   **14** 615 ÷ 20   **15** 801 ÷ 178   **16** 560 ÷ 30

17 1,026 ÷ 93   **18** 902 ÷ 41   **19** 120 ÷ 16   **20** 405 ÷ 45

21 950 ÷ 76   **22** 308 ÷ 12   **23** 1,824 ÷ 60   **24** 279 ÷ 30

25 1,682 ÷ 40   **26** 564 ÷ 20   **27** 732 ÷ 24   **28** 572 ÷ 104

29 1,890 ÷ 315   **30** 756 ÷ 168   **31** 370 ÷ 296   **32** 572 ÷ 176

Name _____

Solve.

1 402 x 9   **2** 256 ÷ 6   **3** 82 x 31   **4** 703 x 9

5 846 ÷ 4   **6** 901 x 51   **7** 186 ÷ 16   **8** 442 x 17

9 510 ÷ 20   **10** 234 ÷ 15   **11** 164 x 57   **12** 945 ÷ 18

13 489 x 22   **14** 434 ÷ 56   **15** 722 x 35   **16** 1,320 ÷ 16

17 729 ÷ 36   **18** 369 x 9   **19** 463 ÷ 25   **20** 501 x 86

21 740 ÷ 57   **22** 21 x 749   **23** 635 x 13   **24** 803 x 18

25 17 x 602   **26** 560 ÷ 42   **27** 27 x 809   **28** 2,500 ÷ 205

29 602 ÷ 35   **30** 1,600 ÷ 24   **31** 1,004 ÷ 40   **32** 38 x 951

Solve.

1. 777 x 4

2. 260 ÷ 4

3. 513 x 3

4. 838 ÷ 8

5. 646 ÷ 20

6. 970 x 5

7. 189 x 9

8. 518 ÷ 6

9. 614 x 14

10. 340 x 170

11. 624 ÷ 26

12. 1,512 ÷ 60

13. 8,421 ÷ 401

14. 6,500 ÷ 8

15. 4,357 ÷ 8

16. 358 x 16

17. 19,314 ÷ 74

18. 1,776 ÷ 80

19. 408 x 57

20. 305 ÷ 25

21. 928 x 29

22. 2,190 ÷ 20

23. 6,520 ÷ 40

24. 402 x 101

25. 205 x 63

26. 770 ÷ 42

27. 599 x 84

28. 2,815 ÷ 55

29. 9,911 ÷ 33

30. 904 x 30

31. 7,840 ÷ 80

32. 1,599 ÷ 123

Name _____

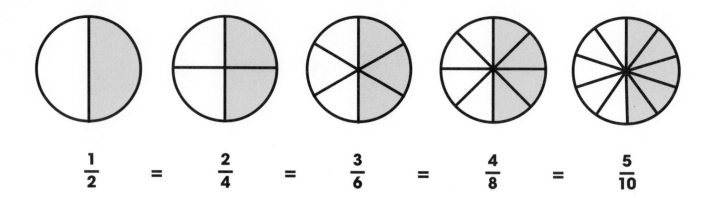

$$\frac{1}{2} \quad = \quad \frac{2}{4} \quad = \quad \frac{3}{6} \quad = \quad \frac{4}{8} \quad = \quad \frac{5}{10}$$

1											
$\frac{1}{2}$						$\frac{1}{2}$					
$\frac{1}{6}$		$\frac{1}{6}$		$\frac{1}{6}$		$\frac{1}{6}$		$\frac{1}{6}$		$\frac{1}{6}$	
$\frac{1}{12}$	$\frac{1}{12}$	$\frac{1}{12}$	$\frac{1}{12}$	$\frac{1}{12}$	$\frac{1}{12}$	$\frac{1}{12}$	$\frac{1}{12}$	$\frac{1}{12}$	$\frac{1}{12}$	$\frac{1}{12}$	$\frac{1}{12}$

1							
$\frac{1}{2}$				$\frac{1}{2}$			
$\frac{1}{4}$		$\frac{1}{4}$		$\frac{1}{4}$		$\frac{1}{4}$	
$\frac{1}{8}$	$\frac{1}{8}$	$\frac{1}{8}$	$\frac{1}{8}$	$\frac{1}{8}$	$\frac{1}{8}$	$\frac{1}{8}$	$\frac{1}{8}$

1									
$\frac{1}{5}$		$\frac{1}{5}$		$\frac{1}{5}$		$\frac{1}{5}$		$\frac{1}{5}$	
$\frac{1}{10}$	$\frac{1}{10}$	$\frac{1}{10}$	$\frac{1}{10}$	$\frac{1}{10}$	$\frac{1}{10}$	$\frac{1}{10}$	$\frac{1}{10}$	$\frac{1}{10}$	$\frac{1}{10}$

Common Core Mathematics Grade 5 • ©2012 Newmark Learning, LLC

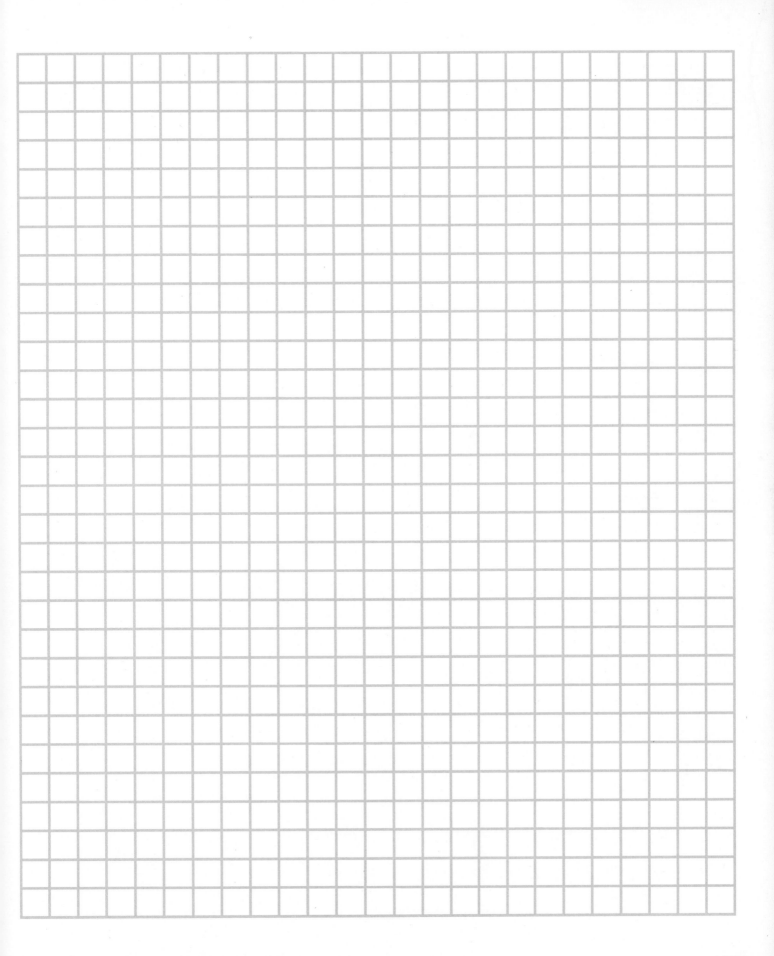

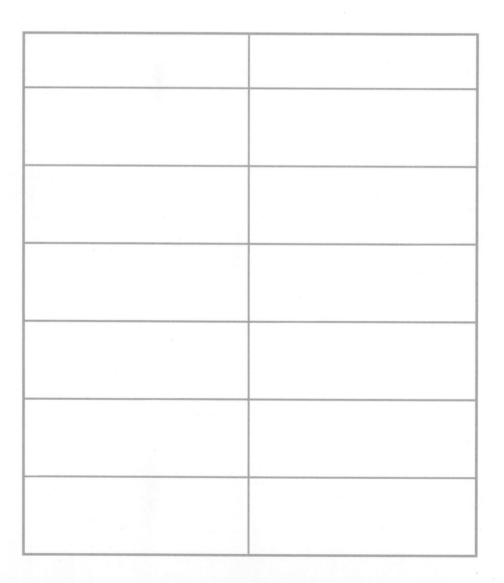

Answer Key • Units 1–2

Unit 1 (p. 7) •
1. 26
2. 10
3. 4
4. 9
5. 11
6. 12
7. 40
8. 13

Unit 1 (p. 8) ••
1. 15
2. 48
3. 8
4. 7
5. 28
6. 7
7. 15
8. 41
9. 35
10. 1
11. 30
12. 9

Unit 1 (p. 9) •••
1. 17
2. 38
3. 100
4. 1
5. 16
6. 14
7. 1,420
8. 33
9. 80
10. 151
11. 93
12. 29.5
13. 48
14. 93
15. 104
16. 144
17. 26
18. 87
19. 78
20. 11

Unit 1 (p. 10)
Word Problems
Answers will vary.
1. 42
2. 17
3. 85
4. 64
5. 12
6. $304
7. B
8. C

Unit 2 (p. 12) •
1. 4×16
2. $11 - 6$
3. $8 - 5$
4. 4×8
5. $3 + 4$
6. $9 - 6$

Unit 2 (p. 13) ••
1. $5 \times (8 - 6)$
2. $9 \times (5 + 3)$
3. $10 \times (12 - 7)$
4. $(4 \times 6) - 8$
5. $(3 \times 7) + 16$
6. $(5 \times 9) - 7$
7. $(2 + 4) + 12$
8. $(30 \div 5) + 14$
9. $(8 \times 6) + 7$
10. $(12 \times 3) - 6$
11. $(9 \times 10) + 11$
12. $(16 - 4) \div 6$

Unit 2 (p. 14) •••
1. $(12 + 9) \div 3$
2. $(17 - 9) \times 3$
3. $(7 + 9) \times 4$
4. $(6 \times 7) + 5$
5. $(8 \times 4) + 7$
6. $(5 \times 7) - 9$
7. $(28 \div 4) + 3$
8. $(28 + 2) - 7$
9. $(9 \times 19) + 5$
10. $(14 \div 7) + 11$
11. $(2 \times 5) \times 6$
12. $(42 - 30) \times 3$
13. $(50 - 17) + 7$
14. $(9 \times 8) \div 6$
15. $(14 + 22) \div 9$
16. $(42 - 34) \div 4$
17. $(17 - 9) \times 4$
18. $(23 + 7) \div 5$
19. $(13 \times 2) - 8$
20. $(45 + 11) \times 2$

Unit 2 (p. 15)
Word Problems
1. $(19 - 13) \times 5 = 30$
2. $(12 \times 5) - 17 = 43$
3. $(28 \div 7) + 4 = 8$
4. $(24 + 12) \div 9 = 4$
5. $3(11 + 4) + 5 = 50$
6. $(5 \times 6) + (3 \times 7) = 51$
7. A
8. C

Answer Key • Units 3–4

Unit 3 (p. 17) •
1. 10, 5; 3, 2, 1
2. 6, 8; 18, 24
3. 6, 4; 12, 8
4. multiply by 2; x + 2; y + 4
5. divide by 6; x – 6; y – 1

Unit 3 (p. 18) ••
1. 10, 12, 14
2. x: 18, 16; y: 10, 9, 8
3. x: 4, 5; y: 5, 10, 15, 20, 25
4. x: 24, 18, 12; y: 24, 20, 16, 12, 8
5. x: 10, 20, 30, 40, 50; y: 20, 40, 60, 80, 100
6. x: 15, 0; y: 40, 35, 30, 25, 20
7. x: 40, 50; y: 15, 30, 45, 60, 75
8. x: 33, 30, 27, 24, 21; y: 12, 11, 10, 9, 8

Unit 3 (p. 19) •••
1. 6, 9, (4, 12)
2. 2, 4, (12, 6), (16, 8)
3. (4, 12), (3, 9), (2, 6), (1, 3)
4. Answers may vary.
5. Answers may vary.
6. Answers may vary.
7. Answers may vary.
8. Answers may vary.
9. Answers may vary.
10. Answers may vary.

Unit 3 (p. 20)
Word Problems
1. double x; x + 3; y + 6
2. double x; x – 2; y – 4
3. 3x; x + 5; y + 15
4. x ÷ 3; x – 3; y – 1
5. 5x; x + 1; y + 5
6. x ÷ 4; x – 4; y – 1
7. C
8. D

Unit 4 (p. 22) •
1. 103.9
2. 40.567
3. 2.13
4. eighteen and six-hundredths
5. ten and thirteen-hundredths
6. 100 + 40 + 5/10

Unit 4 (p. 23) ••
1. 20 + 4 + 7/10 + 6/100; twenty-four and seventy-six hundredths
2. 20 + 1 + 3/100 + 5/1,000; twenty-one and thirty-five thousandths
3. 400 + 4/100; four hundred and four-hundredths
4. 100 + 20 + 1 + 6/100; one hundred twenty-one and six-hundredths
5. 305.5; 300 + 5 + 5/10
6. 718.012; 700 + 10 + 8 + 1/100 + 2/1,000
7. 99.83; ninety-nine and eighty-three hundredths
8. 300 + 4/10; three hundred and four-tenths

Unit 4 (p. 24) •••
1. 6 + 1/10 + 7/100; six and seventeen-hundredths
2. 35.2; thirty-five and two-tenths
3. 4.579; four and five hundred seventy-nine thousandths
4. 802.06; 800 + 2 + 6/100
5. 200 + 6 + 4/100 + 7/1,000; two hundred six and forty-seven thousandths
6. 70 + 4 + 2/10 + 1/100; seventy-four and twenty-one hundredths
7. 8 + 9/100 + 6/1,000; eight and ninety-six thousandths
8. 20.62; 20 + 6/10 + 2/100
9. 95.4; 90 + 5 + 4/10
10. 605.03; six hundred five and three-hundredths

Unit 4 (p. 25)
Word Problems
1. 500 + 10 + 4/10 + 1/1,000
2. 352.4
3. ten and seven-tenths
4. 701.001
5. two hundred fifty-seven and five hundred seventy-two thousandths
6. 900 + 1 + 7/100 + 5/1,000
7. A
8. D

Answer Key • Units 5–8

Unit 5 (p. 27) •
1. 9,000
2. 0.009
3. 1,500; 15,000
4. 720, 7,200, 72,000
5. 0.4; 0.04
6. 3.75; 0.375

Unit 5 (p. 28) ••
1. 2,100
2. 0.005
3. 63; 630
4. 1.07; 0.107
5. 4,320; 43,200; 432,000
6. 90.8; 908; 9,080
7. 86
8. 451
9. 0.033
10. 750
11. 0.0341
12. 92,800

Unit 5 (p. 29) •••
1. 9,430; 94,300; 943,000
2. 7,120; 71,200; 712,000
3. 6.3; 0.63; 0.063
4. 543.3; 54.33; 5.433
5. 4.32
6. 608
7. 285
8. 0.027
9. 25.1
10. 330
11. 745
12. 2.78
13. 0.0219
14. 97.004
15. 80,100
16. 0.5094
17. 0.65
18. 37,750

Unit 5 (p. 30)
Word Problems
1. 339
2. 5,420
3. 109.7
4. 20,000
5. 2.093
6. 700.98
7. B
8. C

Unit 6 (p. 32) •
1. 0.5 is less than 0.7.
2. 0.58 is less than 0.59.
3. 0.094 is greater than 0.049.
4. 0.218 is less than 0.318.
5. 0.073 is greater than 0.013.
6. 1.212 is greater than 1.021.

Unit 6 (p. 33) ••
1. <
2. >
3. <
4. >
5. <
6. =
7. <
8. <
9. >
10. <

Unit 6 (p. 34) •••
1. >
2. <
3. <
4. <
5. <
6. =
7. <
8. >
9. <
10. <
11. >
12. >
13. <
14. >
15. =
16. >

Unit 6 (p. 35)
Word Problems
1. Answers may vary.
2. Answers may vary.
3. Answers may vary.
4. Answers may vary.
5. Alicia
6. cheddar
7. D
8. C

Unit 7 (p. 37) •
1. 5
2. 37
3. 25
4. 4
5. 4
6. 39

Unit 7 (p. 38) ••
1. 8.5
2. 19.1
3. 5.3
4. 61.9
5. 8.6
6. 1.6
7. 15.1
8. 20.4
9. 6.5
10. 0.8

Unit 7 (p. 39) •••
1. 3.46
2. 0.3
3. 40.26
4. 61.90
5. 8.53
6. 81.41
7. 7.60
8. 0.89
9. 0.97
10. 1.09
11. 1.06
12. 4.51

Unit 7 (p. 40)
Word Problems
1. 31.8
2. 1.5
3. 20.1
4. 98.04
5. 5.2
6. 76.98
7. B
8. A

Unit 8 (p. 42) •
1. 546
2. 238
3. 1,208
4. 1,827
5. 1,812
6. 2,135
7. 234
8. 6,870
9. 3,045
10. 12,006

Unit 8 (p. 43) ••
1. 800
2. 1,188
3. 372
4. 1,500
5. 2,793
6. 5,550
7. 13,120
8. 12,798
9. 23,370
10. 12,782
11. 20,928
12. 38,050
13. 34,701

Unit 8 (p. 44) •••
1. 2,968
2. 2,720
3. 1,400
4. 4,320
5. 1,168
6. 1,650
7. 931
8. 2,376
9. 6,058
10. 27,590
11. 2,233
12. 15,980
13. 13,146
14. 11,900
15. 18,383
16. 9,984
17. 16,191
18. 14,314
19. 7,843
20. 8,436
21. 10,080
22. 10,530
23. 7,347
24. 34,003

Unit 8 (p. 45)
Word Problems
1. $648
2. 624 miles
3. 33,998 sq meters
4. 10,725 toys
5. 17,856 pages
6. 471,600 meters
7. A
8. B

Answer Key • Units 9–11

Unit 9 (p. 47) •
1. 9
2. 6
3. 30
4. 61
5. 206

Unit 9 (p. 48) ••
1. 242
2. 13
3. 21
4. 27
5. 63
6. 163
7. 181
8. 297
9. 1,618 R1
10. 2,738

Unit 9 (p. 49) •••
1. 120 R4
2. 67
3. 4,491
4. 27
5. 122 R1
6. 89
7. 21 R3
8. 1,541
9. 405 R1
10. 142 R1
11. 25 R1
12. 257
13. 163
14. 154
15. 114 R2
16. 59
17. 101 R4
18. 251 R1
19. 81 R4
20. 118 R2
21. 938 R5
22. 883
23. 1,456 R5
24. 1,266

Unit 9 (p. 50)
Word Problems
1. 131
2. 12 containers
3. 96 meters
4. 320 gallons
5. 345 miles
6. 586 tickets
7. B
8. C

Unit 10 (p. 52) •
1. 9
2. 2
3. 25
4. 3
5. 19
6. 40
7. 206

Unit 10 (p. 53) ••
1. 29
2. 6
3. 22
4. 8
5. 22
6. 25
7. 113
8. 17
9. 30
10. 214
11. 71
12. 15
13. 70
14. 26 R27
15. 160 R22
16. 35 R13

Unit 10 (p. 54) •••
1. 195
2. 100 R6
3. 17
4. 647
5. 37
6. 89
7. 78
8. 25
9. 410
10. 86
11. 33
12. 425
13. 206
14. 200 R33
15. 240
16. 245
17. 108 R28
18. 37 R6
19. 523
20. 95
21. 201
22. 163
23. 131
24. 1,520

Unit 10 (p. 55)
Word Problems
1. 16 seats
2. 31 feet
3. 291 miles per minute
4. 86 feet
5. 465 pounds
6. 128 cubic feet
7. C
8. D

Unit 11 (p. 57) •
1. 0.61
2. 1.42
3. 0.92
4. 1.1
5. 0.43
6. 0.09

Unit 11 (p. 58) ••
1. 0.88
2. 0.79
3. 8.77
4. 1.02
5. 0.8
6. 1.12
7. 1.05
8. 1.28
9. 0.14
10. 0.59
11. 3.88
12. 2.91
13. 2.29
14. 8.45

Unit 11 (p. 59) •••
1. 2.08
2. 1.88
3. 5.17
4. 40.32
5. 25.56
6. 3.16
7. 3.72
8. 40.61
9. 3.9
10. 13.9
11. 6.91
12. 6.96
13. 7.68
14. 12.7
15. 0.66
16. 3.2
17. 6.8
18. 11.11
19. 6.67
20. 2.04
21. 9.55
22. 12.82
23. 0.38
24. 470.49

Unit 11 (p. 60)
Word Problems
1. 14.82
2. 0.98
3. $1.01
4. $1.25
5. 15.12 pounds
6. 0.63 feet
7. A
8. D

Answer Key • Units 12–14

Unit 12 (p. 62) •
1. 0.2
2. 3.57
3. 0.18
4. 0.21
5. 0.905
6. 2.4

Unit 12 (p. 63) ••
1. 1.61
2. 0.45
3. 1.08
4. 0.084
5. 7.8
6. 0.0604
7. 4.95
8. 0.361
9. 0.11
10. 5.92
11. 0.809
12. 67.545
13. 0.036
14. 2.015
15. 0.6
16. 0.1104

Unit 12 (p. 64) •••
1. 1.5
2. 2.08
3. 11.853
4. 0.1256
5. 0.9
6. 0.9
7. 11.803
8. 0.1416
9. 1.92
10. 0.327
11. 0.391
12. 0.1089
13. 1.65
14. 2.08
15. 4.036
16. 0.1245
17. 49.86
18. 9.99
19. 0.0624
20. 4.151
21. 16.2
22. 70.07
23. 40.42
24. 1.8072

Unit 12 (p. 65)
Word Problems
1. 3.333
2. 28.112
3. $10.50
4. $4.36
5. 7.5 minutes
6. 3.5 cups
7. B
8. A

Unit 13 (p. 67) •
1. 0.4
2. 0.3
3. 1.53
4. 13.4
5. 8
6. 4.4

Unit 13 (p. 68) ••
1. 40.3
2. 0.81
3. 8
4. 10.4
5. 51
6. 1.04
7. 21
8. 0.69
9. 19.5
10. 78
11. 36.5
12. 0.3
13. 30
14. 21
15. 4.93
16. 0.01

Unit 13 (p. 69) •••
1. 0.36
2. 30
3. 7
4. 6.775
5. 0.05
6. 86
7. 6.2
8. 70
9. 3.92
10. 12.25
11. 8.1
12. 3.7
13. 5.85
14. 2.5
15. 1.45
16. 0.2
17. 35
18. 18.55
19. 41.25
20. 79
21. 1.5
22. 6.4
23. 505.5
24. 6.6

Unit 13 (p. 70)
Word Problems
1. 5.6
2. 4.25
3. $9.65
4. $6.99
5. 93 cans
6. 30.2 ounces
7. C
8. A

Unit 14 (p. 72) •
1. 4/6 or 2/3
2. 7/8
3. 5/6
4. 5/8
5. 8/6 or 1 1/3
6. 7/9

Unit 14 (p. 73) ••
1. 5/6
2. 3/4
3. 1 1/4
4. 1 1/3
5. 1
6. 2/3
7. 1 1/8
8. 7/8

Unit 14 (p. 74) •••
1. 1/2, <
2. 1 1/4, >
3. 7/10, <
4. 5/8, <
5. 7/9, <
6. 9/10, <
7. 5/8, <
8. 1 3/8, >
9. 32/35, <
10. 11/12, <
11. 13/15, <
12. 5/6, <
13. 1 1/10, >
14. 13/24, <
15. 19/21, <
16. 39/40, <

Unit 14 (p. 75)
Word Problems
1. 7/8
2. 13/20
3. 1 1/35
4. 5 pages
5. 3/8
6. 9 sections
7. D
8. A

Answer Key • Units 15–18

Unit 15 (p. 77) •
1. 1/6
2. 3/8
3. 1/3
4. 1/2
5. 2/9
6. 5/12

Unit 15 (p. 78) ••
1. 1/6
2. 1/4
3. 3/10
4. 1/3
5. 0
6. 1/6
7. 5/8
8. 1/8

Unit 15 (p. 79) •••
1. 1/6   2. 1/4
3. 1/2   4. 3/8
5. 5/9   6. 0
7. 3/8   8. 1/8
9. 18/35   10. 1/4
11. 7/15   12. 1/15
13. 3/10   14. 11/24
15. 3/14   16. 31/40

Unit 15 (p. 80)
Word Problems
1. 2/5
2. 9/20
3. 17/40
4. 2/5
5. 6 slices
6. 3 sections
7. A
8. B

Unit 16 (p. 82) •
1. 3
2. 2
3. 3
4. 5
5. 2
6. 4

Unit 16 (p. 83) ••
1. 3; 3   2. 3
3. 2   4. 2
5. 4   6. 4
7. 10   8. 6
9. 9 3/5
10. 25/7 or 3 4/7

Unit 16 (p. 84) •••
1. 4   2. 4
3. 7 1/5   4. 8 1/3
5. 4 1/2   6. 6
7. 6   8. 4 4/5
9. 4   10. 2 4/5
11. 4 2/3   12. 5 1/2
13. 2 1/10 14. 2 1/2
15. 6   16. 7 1/7

Unit 16 (p. 85)
Word Problems
1. 10 2/3 pounds
2. 9 ounces
3. 2 1/2 square meters
4. 13 1/8 meters
5. 225 stamps
6. 39 cheesecakes
7. C
8. C

Unit 17 (p. 87) •
1. 1/6
2. 1/8
3. 1/12
4. 2/5
5. 1/6
6. 3/32

Unit 17 (p. 88) ••
1. 1/3   2. 5/16
3. 1/5   4. 3/8
5. 5/8   6. 1/20
7. 7/12   8. 1/7
9. 3/16   10. 5/54

Unit 17 (p. 89) •••
1. 1/6   2. 4/9
3. 5/32   4. 5/42
5. 3/16   6. 2/15
7. 9/16   8. 3/40
9. 1/15   10. 1/4
11. 1/6   12. 5/9
13. 3/7   14. 3/10
15. 1/10   16. 27/100

Unit 17 (p. 90)
Word Problems
1. 1/4 gallon
2. 1/3 pound
3. 3/10 km
4. 5/9 yard
5. 3/5
6. 2/5
7. C
8. D

Unit 18 (p. 92) •
1. 3/8
2. 5/16
3. 8/15
4. 7/12

Unit 18 (p. 93) ••
1. 1 5/6   2. 1 1/3
3. 3/4   4. 9/16
5. 3 9/32   6. 1
7. 19/24   8. 18/25
9. 1 7/10   10. 8 2/15

Unit 18 (p. 94) •••
1. 3 3/4   2. 7 5/16
3. 7 7/9   4. 4
5. 3 2/3   6. 3
7. 7   8. 3 3/5
9. 9 7/20
10. 8 17/24
11. 11 23/27
12. 20 4/5

Unit 18 (p. 95)
Word Problems
1. 1 7/8 cups
2. 7/8 acre
3. 2/3 pound
4. 82 2/3 square yards
5. 36 5/6 square meters
6. 4 2/5 pounds
7. D
8. A

Answer Key • Units 19–22

Unit 19 (p. 97) •
1. 6
2. 12
3. 6
4. 10
5. 1/16
6. 1/9

Unit 19 (p. 98) ••
1. 1/6
2. 32
3. 10
4. 1/12
5. 1/12
6. 1/3
7. 1/21
8. 2/15
9. 1/10
10. 1/5

Unit 19 (p. 99) •••
1. 2/5
2. 1/3
3. 3/4
4. 1/5
5. 5/8
6. 1/2
7. 1 1/3
8. 1 2/7
9. 2 1/6
10. 5 2/5
11. 4 1/4
12. 3 3/5
13. 5 1/2
14. 3 1/2
15. 5 1/3
16. 10 2/5

Unit 19 (p. 100)
Word Problems
1. 20 bowls
2. 1/6 kilogram
3. 7/16 mile
4. 40 bags
5. 5 times
6. 12 days
7. D
8. C

Unit 20 (p. 102) •
1. 30
2. 5
3. 8,000
4. 0.085
5. 0.17
6. 0.6

Unit 20 (p. 103) ••
1. 0.02
2. 1.3
3. 9,000
4. 0.05
5. 4.02
6. 0.007
7. 30,000
8. 10.5

Unit 20 (p. 104) •••
1. 0.005
2. 0.36
3. 2.85
4. 1.9
5. 0.07
6. 0.305
7. 6,000
8. 807,000
9. 25,500
10. 1.1
11. 0.45
12. 0.01

Unit 20 (p. 105)
Word Problems
1. 150,000 mL
2. 48.567 metric tons
3. 250 boards
4. 17.5 km
5. 9.3 kg
6. 1.45 km
7. D
8. C

Unit 21 (p. 107) •
1. 4
2. 11
3. 18
4. 32
5. 144
6. 150
7. 3 yd 1 ft
8. 90 yd 2 ft

Unit 21 (p. 108) ••
1. 3
2. 5
3. 4
4. 6 lbs 4 oz
5. 30,000
6. 64,000
7. 3,000
8. 6,500
9. 1.75 or 1 3/4
10. 2.5 or 2 1/2
11. 64,000
12. 4.0625 or 4 1/16

Unit 21 (p. 109) •••
Check students' work.
1. 6
2. 1/2
3. 12 1/4
4. 16
5. 4
6. 5
7. 8
8. 100
9. 108
10. 128
11. 53
12. 40

Unit 21 (p. 110)
Word Problems
1. 5 ft
2. 168 ft
3. 10 servings
4. 4 cups
5. 12 presents
6. 3,570 yd
7. B
8. D

Unit 22 (p. 112) •
1. weights of chestnuts
2. Information is stacked in lines.
3. 5
4. 2 ounces
5. 3.5 ounces
6. 21

Unit 22 (p. 113) ••
1. how fast athletes race
2. 13
3. 18
4. 11 seconds
5. 14 seconds
6. 3 seconds
7. 12.5 seconds
8. 12.6 seconds

Unit 22 (p. 114) •••
1. length of mealworm beetles
2. 1 1/4 cm
3. 16
4. 1 1/4
5. 2 cm
6. 3/4 cm
7. 1 1/4 cm
8. 1 3/8 cm

Unit 22 (p. 115)
Word Problems
1. Check students' work.
2. growth of plants
3. 3/4 cm
4. 12
5. 2 cm
6. B
7. B

Answer Key • Units 23–27

Unit 23 (p. 117) •
1. 9 cubic units
2. 10 cubic units
3. 12 cubic units
4. 20 cubic units

Unit 23 (p. 118) ••
1. 8 cubic cm
2. 18 cubic cm
3. 12 cubic cm
4. 16 cubic cm
5. 18 cubic cm
6. 36 cubic cm

Unit 23 (p. 119) •••
1. 27 cubic units
2. 48 cubic units
3. 12 cubic units
4. 18 cubic units
5. 24 cubic units
6. 20 cubic units
7. 24 cubic units
8. 36 cubic units

Unit 23 (p. 120)
Word Problems
1. 24 cubic units
2. 36 cubic units
3. 18 cubic cm
4. 20 cubic in
5. 64 cubic units
6. 12 cubic units
7. C   8. C

Unit 24 (p. 122) •
1. 64 cubic cm
2. 24 cubic m
3. 48 cubic ft
4. 84 cubic ft

Unit 24 (p. 123) ••
1. 180 cubic cm
2. 40 cubic ft
3. 84 cubic m
4. 144 cubic cm
5. 1,000 cubic m
6. 30 cubic m

Unit 24 (p. 124) •••
1. 80 cubic cm
2. 200 cubic ft
3. 3 m   4. 2 cm
5. 5 cm   6. 3 in
7. 3 cm   8. 8 cm
9. 4 units   10. 5 cm

Unit 24 (p. 125)
Word Problems
1. 80 cubic in
2. 90 cubic units
3. 96 cubic ft
4. 360 cubic cm
5. 512 cubic in
6. 2,772 cubic in
7. D   8. D

Unit 25 (p. 127) •
1. home
2. playground
3. soccer field
4. school
5. library
6. post office

Unit 25 (p. 128) ••
1. (1, 1)   2. (3, 11)
3. (7, 9)   4. (3, 6)
5. (8, 2)   6. (6, 3)
7. (9, 7)   8. (11, 3)
9. (2, 8)   10. (13, 12)

Unit 25 (p. 129) •••
1. (2, 2)   2. (2, 5)
3. (5, 5)   4. (5, 2)
5. (4, 9)   6. (9, 9)
7. (9, 7)   8. (13, 3)
9. (13, 1)   10. (9, 1)
11. (9, 3)   12. (11, 5)
13. square   14. triangle
15. pentagon

Unit 25 (p. 130)
Word Problems
1. (5, 3)
2. (3, 5)
3. (5, 9)
4. U
5. triangle
6. S, T, U, V
7. D   8. B

Unit 26 (p. 132) •
Check students' work.

Unit 26 (p. 133) ••
Check students' work.

Unit 26 (p. 134) •••
Check students' work.
7. trapezoid

Unit 26 (p. 135)
Word Problems
1-4. Check students' work.
5. B   6. C

Unit 27 (p. 137) •
Check students' work.

Unit 27 (p. 138) ••
Check students' work

Unit 27 (p. 139) •••
Check students' work

Unit 27 (p. 140)
Word Problems
1. polygon,
   parallelogram,
   equilateral
2. rectangle
3–4. Check students' work.
5. D   6. B

Answer Key • Fluency Practice

p. 141

1. 572	**5.** 1,180	**9.** 12,656	**13.** 6,119	**17.** 14,219	**21.** 14,448	**25.** 14,223	**29.** 17,220
2. 1,632	**6.** 231	**10.** 11,808	**14.** 10,370	**18.** 25,888	**22.** 4,536	**26.** 6,825	**30.** 30,456
3. 36,114	**7.** 1,569	**11.** 38,661	**15.** 6,528	**19.** 29,304	**23.** 15,921	**27.** 49,245	**31.** 111,864
4. 130,175	**8.** 1,624	**12.** 7,880	**16.** 11,419	**20.** 14,084	**24.** 13,184	**28.** 6,012	**32.** 127,712

p. 142

1. 4,011	**5.** 1,692	**9.** 6,100	**13.** 11,560	**17.** 22,848	**21.** 8,066	**25.** 8,822	**29.** 43,860
2. 1,410	**6.** 4,855	**10.** 6,460	**14.** 19,800	**18.** 1,776	**22.** 7,980	**26.** 24,584	**30.** 4,944
3. 1,542	**7.** 1,557	**11.** 832	**15.** 6,596	**19.** 28,098	**23.** 31,600	**27.** 48, 528	**31.** 505,521
4. 5,072	**8.** 1,848	**12.** 11,529	**16.** 9,900	**20.** 28,210	**24.** 80,200	**28.** 11,250	**32.** 43,778

p. 143

1. 2,124	**5.** 23,650	**9.** 18,120	**13.** 9,315	**17.** 57,908	**21.** 37,595	**25.** 83,013	**29.** 191,835
2. 9,135	**6.** 31,537	**10.** 11,820	**14.** 12,220	**18.** 19,228	**22.** 3,696	**26.** 21,840	**30.** 127,512
3. 1,652	**7.** 11,726	**11.** 3,465	**15.** 6,942	**19.** 9,085	**23.** 15,120	**27.** 17,568	**31.** 113,072
4. 5,120	**8.** 12,948	**12.** 24,969	**16.** 12,650	**20.** 9,225	**24.** 7,980	**28.** 44,200	**32.** 86,697

p. 144

1. 82	**5.** 106.5	**9.** 61	**13.** 7.5	**17.** 19	**21.** 12	**25.** 5.5	**29.** 12
2. 40	**6.** 194	**10.** 2	**14.** 75	**18.** 14.8	**22.** 40	**26.** 10.5	**30.** 8.18
3. 171	**7.** 21	**11.** 6	**15.** 21	**19.** 28	**23.** 12.8	**27.** 11	**31.** 9.625
4. 79.5	**8.** 50.5	**12.** 4	**16.** 90	**20.** 23	**24.** 80.2	**28.** 40.9	**32.** 13

p. 145

1. 236	**5.** 9.5	**9.** 60	**13.** 11.2	**17.** 11.03	**21.** 12.5	**25.** 42.05	**29.** 6
2. 40.6	**6.** 51	**10.** 12.5	**14.** 30.75	**18.** 22	**22.** 25.67	**26.** 28.2	**30.** 4.5
3. 103.25	**7.** 13	**11.** 12	**15.** 4.5	**19.** 7.5	**23.** 30.4	**27.** 30.5	**31.** 1.25
4. 12.5	**8.** 6	**12.** 30	**16.** 18.67	**20.** 9	**24.** 9.3	**28.** 5.5	**32.** 3.25

p. 146

1. 3,618	**5.** 211.5	**9.** 25.5	**13.** 10,758	**17.** 20.25	**21.** 12.98	**25.** 10,234	**29.** 17.2
2. 42.67	**6.** 45,951	**10.** 15.6	**14.** 7.75	**18.** 3,321	**22.** 15,729	**26.** 13.33	**30.** 66.67
3. 2,542	**7.** 11.625	**11.** 9,348	**15.** 25,270	**19.** 18.52	**23.** 8,255	**27.** 21,843	**31.** 25.1
4. 6,327	**8.** 7,514	**12.** 52.5	**16.** 82.5	**20.** 43,086	**24.** 14,454	**28.** 12.2	**32.** 36,138

p. 147

1. 3,108	**5.** 32.3	**9.** 8,596	**13.** 21	**17.** 261	**21.** 26,912	**25.** 12,915	**29.** 300.33
2. 65	**6.** 4,850	**10.** 57,800	**14.** 812.5	**18.** 22.2	**22.** 109.5	**26.** 18.33	**30.** 27,120
3. 1,539	**7.** 1,701	**11.** 24	**15.** 544.63	**19.** 23,256	**23.** 163	**27.** 50,316	**31.** 98
4. 104.75	**8.** 86.33	**12.** 25.2	**16.** 5,728	**20.** 12.2	**24.** 40,602	**28.** 51.18	**32.** 13

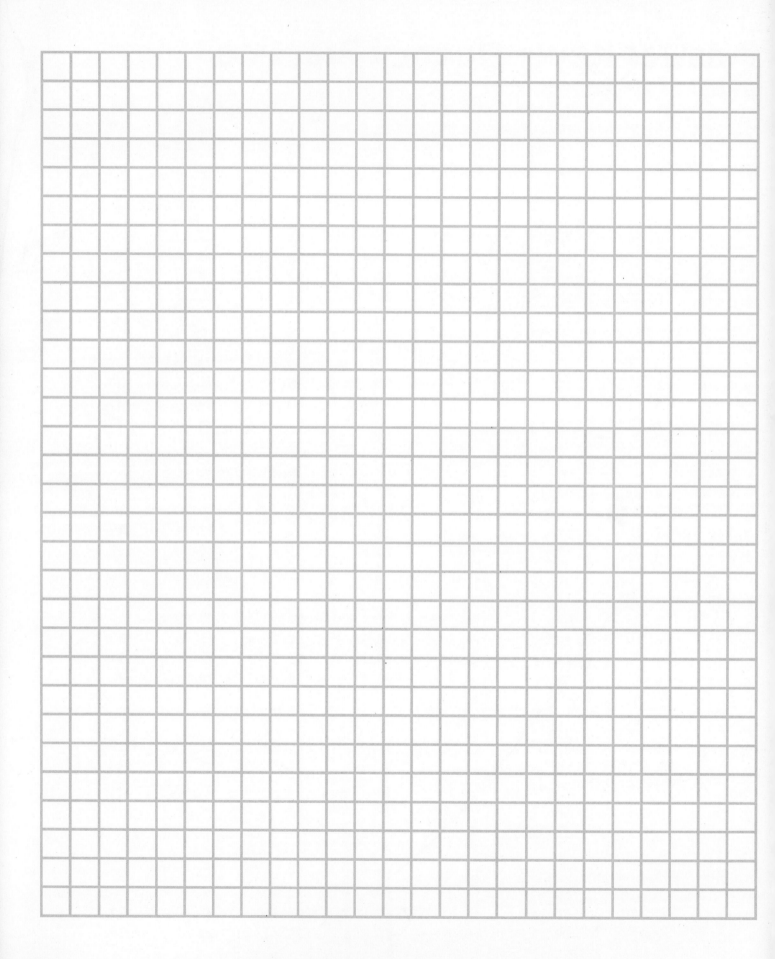